Complete
Mechanics
for Cambridge International AS & A Level

Second Edition

Phil Crossley
Jim Fensom
Martin Burgess

Oxford excellence for Cambridge AS & A Level

Great Clarendon Street, Oxford, OX2 6DP, United Kingdom

Oxford University Press is a department of the University of Oxford. It furthers
the University's objective of excellence in research, scholarship, and education
by publishing worldwide. Oxford is a registered trade mark of Oxford University
Press in the UK and in certain other countries

British Library Cataloguing in Publication Data
Data available

978-0-19-842519-9

10 9 8

Paper used in the production of this book is a natural, recyclable product made from
wood grown in sustainable forests. The manufacturing process conforms to the
environmental regulations of the country of origin

Printed in India by Thomson Press

*The questions, all example answers and comments that appear in this book were
written by the authors*

Acknowledgements

The publishers would like to thank the following for permissions to use their photographs:

Cover: Antun Hirsman/Shutterstock; **p2:** David Wall/Alamy; **p7:** Current Value/Shutterstock; **p10:** Associated Sports
Photography/Alamy; **p11t:** Image Source/Alamy; **p11b:** Ian Miles-Flashpoint Pictures/Alamy; **p18:** Maxisport/Shutter-
stock; **p24:** Hulton Archive/Stringer/Getty; **p30:** andras_csontos/Shutterstock; **p46b:** OUP/Andrew Fosker/Seconds Left/
REX; **p46t:** OUP/Suwatchai Pluemruetai; **p47t:** OUP/3D Renderings/Shutterstock; **p47b:** Neil Tingle/Alamy; **p48:** SSPL/
Getty Images; **p49:** World History Archive/Alamy; **p50l:** Danny Smythe/Shutterstock; **p50r:** Fedor Selivanov/Shutter-
stock; **p52t:** Francoise de Valera/Shutterstock; **p52b:** Corepics VOF/Shutterstock; **p57:** Irina Kovancova/Shutterstock;
p59: Mesut Dogan/Shutterstock; **p62:** Tupungato/Shutterstock; **p72:** Richard Thornton/Shutterstock; **p88t:** Sciepro/
Science Photo Library; **p88c:** Sebastien Beaucourt/Look at Sciences/Science Photo Library; **p88b:** Mechanik/Shutterstock;
p89t: Claus Lunau/Science Photo Library; **p89b:** ZUMA Press, Inc./Alamy; **p90:** Prisma Bildagentur AG/Alamy; **p95:**
hektR/Shutterstock; **p98:** Germanskydiver/Shutterstock; **p101:** Mitch Gunn/Shutterstock; **p106:** Natursports/Shutter-
stock; **p107:** Georgios Kollidas/Shutterstock; **p113:** Jaroslav Pachy Sr/Shutterstock; **p118:** Science Museum/Science &
Society Picture Library; **p122:** Oleksiy Mark/Shutterstock; **p134t:** RGB Ventures/SuperStock/Alamy; **p134b:** imageBRO-
KER/Alamy; **p135t:** NASA Langley Research Center; **p135b:** LOC Photo/Alamy

Contents

Introduction

About this book

This book has been written to cover the **Cambridge AS & A Level International Mathematics (9709)** course, and is fully aligned to the syllabus.

In addition to the main curriculum content, you will find:

- 'Maths in real-life', showing how principles learned in this course are used in the real world.
- Chapter openers, which outline how each topic in the Cambridge 9709 syllabus is used in real-life.

The book contains the following features:

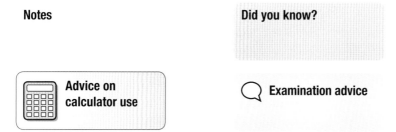

Notes

Did you know?

Advice on calculator use

Examination advice

Throughout the book, you will encounter worked examples and a host of rigorous exercises. The examples show you the important techniques required to tackle questions. The exercises are carefully graded, starting from a basic level and going up to exam standard, allowing you plenty of opportunities to practise your skills. Together, the examples and exercises put maths in a real-world context, with a truly international focus.

At the start of each chapter, you will see a list of objectives that are covered in the chapter. These objectives are drawn from the Cambridge AS & A Level syllabus. Each chapter begins with a *Before you start* section and finishes with a *Summary exercise* and *Chapter summary*, ensuring that you fully understand each topic.

Each chapter contains key mathematical terms to improve understanding, highlighted in colour, with full definitions provided in the Glossary of terms at the end of the book.

The answers given at the back of the book are concise. However, when answering exam-style questions, you should show as many steps in your working as possible. All exam-style questions, as well as *Paper A* and *Paper B*, have been written by the authors.

About the authors

Jim Fensom has many years' experience of teaching and examining mathematics. He has authored a number of books. He recently retired after a career teaching in the UK and Singapore.

Phil Crossley is a senior examiner as well as a teacher at Carre's Grammar School in England. He has many years of experience in teaching and examining mathematics.

Dr Martin Burgess has over nine years' experience in teaching mathematics at secondary level and has also been an expert examiner for an A Level examination board. His PhD is in the field of data mining, specialising in statistical techniques, and he works at Nexus International School in Singapore.

Special thanks to James Nicholson for 'Maths in real-life'.

A note from the authors

The aim of this book is to help students prepare for the Mechanics unit of the Cambridge International AS & A Level Mathematics syllabus, though it may also be found to be useful in providing support material for other AS and A Level courses. The book contains a large number of practice questions, many of which are exam-style.

In writing the book we have drawn on our experiences of teaching mathematics over many years, as well as our experience as examiners.

OXFORD
UNIVERSITY PRESS

Student book & Cambridge syllabus matching grid

ASPIRE
SUCCEED
PROGRESS

Student Book: *Complete Mechanics for Cambridge International AS & A Level*

Syllabus: *Cambridge International AS & A Level Mathematics: Mechanics (9709)*

MECHANICS	Student Book

Syllabus overview for 9709, first examined in 2020.

Mechanics (Paper 4)

Questions set will be mainly numerical, and will aim to test mechanical principles without involving difficult algebra or trigonometry. However, candidates should be familiar in particular with the following trigonometrical results:

$\sin(90° - \theta) = \cos\theta$; $\cos(90° - \theta) = \sin\theta$; $\tan\theta \equiv \dfrac{\sin\theta}{\cos\theta}$; $\sin^2\theta + \cos^2\theta \equiv 1$.

Knowledge of algebraic methods from the content for Paper 1: Pure Mathematics 1 is assumed.

This content list refers to the equilibrium or motion of a 'particle'. Examination questions may involve extended bodies in a 'realistic' context, but these extended bodies should be treated as particles, so any force acting on them is modelled as acting at a single point.

Vector notation will not be used in the question papers.

1. Forces and equilibrium

<table>
<tr><td>• Identify the forces acting in a given situation</td><td>Pages 42–47</td></tr>
<tr><td>• Understand the vector nature of force, and find and use components and resultants</td><td>Pages 42–47</td></tr>
<tr><td>• Use the principle that, when a particle is in equilibrium, the vector sum of the forces acting is zero, or equivalently, that the sum of the components in any direction is zero</td><td>Pages 47–56</td></tr>
<tr><td>• Understand that a contact force between two surfaces can be represented by two components, the normal component and the frictional component</td><td>Pages 73–77</td></tr>
<tr><td>• Use the model of a 'smooth' contact, and understand the limitations of this model</td><td>Pages 73–74</td></tr>
<tr><td>• Understand the concepts of limiting friction and limiting equilibrium; recall the definition of coefficient of friction, and use the relationship $F = \mu R$ or $F \leq \mu R$, as appropriate</td><td>Pages 73–83</td></tr>
<tr><td>• Use Newton's third law</td><td>Pages 57–60</td></tr>
</table>

2. Kinematics of motion in a straight line

<table>
<tr><td>• Understand the concepts of distance and speed as scalar quantities, and of displacement, velocity and acceleration as vector quantities (in one dimension only)</td><td>Pages 2–17, 18–28</td></tr>
<tr><td>• Sketch and interpret displacement–time graphs and velocity–time graphs, and in particular appreciate that:</td><td>Pages 2–17</td></tr>
<tr><td>   – the area under a velocity–time graph represents displacement</td><td>Page 8</td></tr>
<tr><td>   – the gradient of a displacement–time graph represents velocity</td><td>Page 4</td></tr>
<tr><td>   – the gradient of a velocity–time graph represents acceleration</td><td>Page 8</td></tr>
</table>

• Use differentiation and integration with respect to time to solve simple problems concerning displacement, velocity and acceleration (restricted to techniques from the content for Paper 1: Pure Mathematics 1)	Pages 29–37
• Use appropriate formulae for motion with constant acceleration in a straight line	Page 37

3. Momentum

• Use the definition of linear momentum and show understanding of its vector nature	Pages 112–114
• Use the conservation of linear momentum to solve problems that may be modelled as the direct impact of two bodies (including direct impact where the bodies coalesce on impact). Note: knowledge of impulse and the coefficient of restitution is not required	Pages 115–123

4. Newton's laws of motion

• Apply Newton's laws of motion to the linear motion of a particle of constant mass moving under the action of constant forces, which may include friction, tension in an inextensible string and thrust in a connecting rod	Pages 57–72
• Use the relationship between mass and weight	Page 60
• Solve simple problems that may be modelled as the motion of a particle moving vertically or on an inclined plane with constant acceleration	Pages 60–66
• Solve simple problems that may be modelled as the motion of connected particles, e.g. connected by a light inextensible string that may pass over a fixed smooth peg or light pulley	Pages 66–72

5. Energy, work and power

• Understand the concept of the work done by a force, and calculate the work done by a constant force when its point of application undergoes a displacement not necessarily parallel to the force (use of the scalar product is not required)	Pages 86–91
• Understand the concepts of gravitational potential energy and kinetic energy, and use appropriate formulae	Pages 91–92
• Understand and use the relationship between the change in energy of a system and the work done by the external forces, and use in appropriate cases the principle of conservation of energy	Pages 92–101
• Use the definition of power as the rate at which a force does work, and use the relationship between power, force and velocity for a force acting in the direction of motion	Pages 102–106
• Solve problems involving, for example, the instantaneous acceleration of a car moving on a hill with resistance	Pages 106–111

The longest straight stretch of train track in the world is in Australia. It runs from Ooldea, in South Australia, to Loongana, in Western Australia, a distance of 478 km. This section of track is part of the Trans-Australian Railway on which the Indian Pacific line from Sydney, in the East of Australia, to Perth, in the West, runs. It runs though the Nullarbor Plain, an area of flat, almost treeless, arid or semi-arid country that occupies an area of 200 000 square kilometres. The length of the journey is 4352 km one-way, and takes 65 hours. The average speed of trains is 85 km/h and its maximum speed is 115 km/h.

Objectives

Sketch and interpret displacement–time graphs and velocity–time graphs, and in particular appreciate that

- the area under a velocity–time graph represents displacement
- the gradient of a displacement–time graph represents velocity
- the gradient of a velocity–time graph represents acceleration.

Before you start

You should know how to:

1. Calculate the area of rectangles, triangles and trapeziums.

e.g.

2.4 cm

Area = 2.4 × 5
    = 12 cm²

5 cm
2 cm
6.2 cm

Area = 6.2 × 2
    = 12.4 cm²

3 cm
7 cm

Area = $\frac{1}{2}$ (4 + 7) × 3
    = 16.5 cm²

2. Calculate the **gradient** of a straight line.

Use gradient = $\frac{y_2 - y_1}{x_2 - x_1}$. **e.g.** Find the gradient of the line joining (2, 4) and (7, −1).

gradient = $\frac{-1 - 4}{7 - 2} = \frac{-5}{5} = -1$

Skills check:

1. Calculate the area of the shape created between the red line of this graph and the *x*-axis.

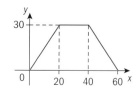

2. Calculate the gradients of these lines.

a)

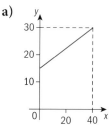

b)

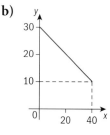

3. Calculate **displacement**, **velocity**, **acceleration** and time using appropriate units (m, m s^{-1}, m s^{-2}, s).

When velocity is constant then the formulae that connect these quantities are as follows:

displacement = velocity × time
e.g. Find the displacement of a particle travelling at 3 m s^{-1} for 5 s.
displacement = 3 × 5 = 15 m

velocity = $\dfrac{\text{displacement}}{\text{time}}$
e.g. Find the velocity when a particle has a displacement of 2.4 m in 3 s.
velocity = $\dfrac{2.4}{3}$ = 0.8 m s^{-1}

time = $\dfrac{\text{displacement}}{\text{velocity}}$
e.g. Find the time taken for a particle to be displaced 15 m with a velocity of 0.6 m s^{-1}.
time = $\dfrac{15}{0.6}$ = 25 s

When acceleration is constant then the formulae that connect these quantities are as follows:

velocity = acceleration × time
e.g. Find the change in velocity when a particle accelerates for 2 s at 24 m s^{-2}.
change in velocity = 24 × 2 = 48 m s^{-1}

acceleration = $\dfrac{\text{velocity}}{\text{time}}$
e.g. Find the acceleration when the velocity of a particle changes from 2 m s^{-1} to 10 m s^{-1} in 12 s.
acceleration = $\dfrac{10-2}{12} = \dfrac{2}{3}$ m s^{-2}

time = $\dfrac{\text{velocity}}{\text{acceleration}}$, **e.g.** Find the time taken for a particle to accelerate to a velocity of 8 m s^{-1} from 3 m s^{-1} when its acceleration is 0.1 m s^{-2}.
time = $\dfrac{5}{0.1}$ = 50 s

3. Find the time taken for a particle travelling
   a) 30 m at a velocity of 5 m s^{-1}
   b) 8 m at a velocity of 0.2 m s^{-1}
   c) 5 m at a velocity of 25 m s^{-1}.

4. Find the displacement of a particle travelling with
   a) a velocity of 12 m s^{-1} for 12 s
   b) a velocity of 0.4 m s^{-1} for 10 s
   c) a velocity of 30 m s^{-1} for 0.5 s.

5. Find the velocity of a particle that has
   a) a displacement of 24 m in 8 s
   b) a displacement of 45 m in 30 s
   c) a displacement of 10 m in 50 s.

6. Find the change in velocity when a particle accelerates at
   a) 10 m s^{-2} for 10 s
   b) 0.2 m s^{-2} for 30 s.

7. Find the acceleration when a particle's velocity changes
   a) from 20 m s^{-1} to 50 m s^{-1} in 10 s
   b) from 44 m s^{-1} to 32 m s^{-1} in 6 s.

8. Find the time taken for a particle to accelerate from 15 m s^{-1} to 60 m s^{-1} at 15 m s^{-2}.

1.1 Displacement–time graphs

A **displacement–time graph** is used to show the motion of a **particle**, in one dimension, along a straight line. We first look at examples where motion follows one or more stages of constant velocity, with the particle moving forwards and backwards along the straight line. In displacement–time graphs, time (t) is shown on the horizontal axis. Displacement is often denoted by s.

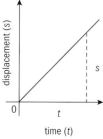

We know that velocity $= \dfrac{\text{displacement}}{\text{time}}$, which can be abbreviated as velocity $= \dfrac{s}{t}$.

> Velocity is the gradient of the displacement–time graph.

Note that the concept of **kinematics**, or straight-line motion, refers to the motion of a particle. A particle has dimensions so small compared with other lengths that its position in space can be represented by a single point. A **body** is an object made up of particles. However, in Example 1, a body (in this case a car) is modelled as a particle for the purpose of the question.

Example 1

A car moves forward on a straight road from a point O, at constant velocity for 20 s, travelling a distance of 60 m. During the next 20 s the car is stationary, remaining 60 m away from O. The car then returns to O, which takes 10 s.

a) **Sketch** a displacement–time graph of the first 50 s of the car's journey.

b) Use the displacement–time graph to find the velocity of the car during each stage of the journey.

. . . .

a)

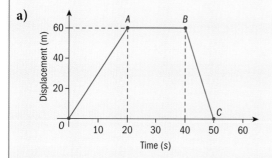

Note: In this example, displacement away from O is regarded as positive; hence, on the return part of the journey, both the displacement and the velocity are negative.

b) Since velocity $= \dfrac{\text{displacement}}{\text{time}}$, the gradient of a displacement–time graph is the velocity.

The gradient of OA is $\dfrac{60}{20} = 3$.
The velocity in the first 20 s is $3\,\text{m s}^{-1}$.

The gradient of AB is 0.
The velocity in the second 20 s is $0\,\text{m s}^{-1}$.

The gradient of BC is $\dfrac{-60}{10} = -6$.
The velocity in the final 10 s is $-6\,\text{m s}^{-1}$.

Exercise 1.1

1. A particle travelling in a straight line, starting from a point O at a velocity of $2\,\mathrm{m\,s^{-1}}$ for $10\,\mathrm{s}$, rests for $20\,\mathrm{s}$ and then returns to O in $5\,\mathrm{s}$.

    a) Sketch the displacement–time graph of the motion of the particle.

    b) What is the velocity of the particle on the return?

2. A car travels along a straight road from a town O. It travels $200\,\mathrm{m}$ at a constant velocity of $20\,\mathrm{m\,s^{-1}}$. It then stops for 5 seconds before returning to the starting point in $8\,\mathrm{s}$.

    a) Sketch a displacement–time graph for the motion of the car.

    b) **Calculate** the velocity on the return section of the journey.

3. A food container in a sushi restaurant travels along a straight track at a velocity of $0.5\,\mathrm{m\,s^{-1}}$ for $10\,\mathrm{s}$. It stops for $10\,\mathrm{s}$ and then continues on its journey at a velocity of $0.6\,\mathrm{m\,s^{-1}}$, coming to a halt after a further $10\,\mathrm{s}$.

    a) Sketch the displacement–time graph for the food container.

    b) Calculate the total distance travelled by the food container.

    Note: In the graphs that follow, displacement (s) is given in metres, and time (t) is in seconds.

4. **Describe** the motion of the particle in the graph. What is the velocity of the particle

    a) in the first 10 seconds

    b) between $t = 10$ and $t = 40$

    c) in the last 30 seconds?

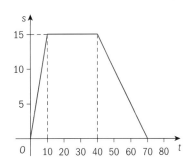

5. Describe the motion of a train moving along a track, as shown in the accompanying graph. What is the velocity of the train

    a) in the first 5 seconds

    b) between $t = 5$ and $t = 20$

    c) in the last 15 seconds?

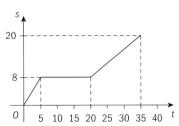

6. Describe the motion of an elevator moving in an elevator shaft, as shown in the graph.

What is the velocity of the elevator

a) in the first 8 seconds

b) between $t = 8$ and $t = 16$

c) in the last 12 seconds?

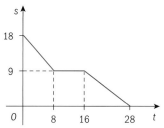

7. In a factory, a piece of steel travels a distance S from O in $40\,s$ on a straight conveyor belt and then returns to O $20\,s$ later as shown in the diagram below.

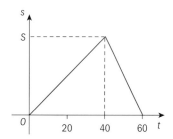

If the initial velocity of the piece of steel is $8\,m\,s^{-1}$, calculate

a) the value of S

b) the velocity of the piece of steel between $t = 40$ and $t = 60$.

8. A particle travels $20\,m$ in a straight line from O in $T\,s$. It remains stationary for a further $T\,s$, and then returns directly to O in $T\,s$ as shown in the graph below.

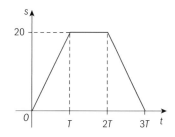

If the initial velocity of the particle is $30\,m\,s^{-1}$, calculate

a) the value of T

b) the time taken to complete the whole journey.

9. The displacement of a particle from O is S m in a time $4T$ s.
   The particle then returns to O as shown in the graph.

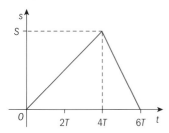

   a) If the initial velocity is $4\,\mathrm{m\,s^{-1}}$, find the velocity on the return.
   b) If the total time taken is $27\,\mathrm{s}$, find the value of S.

10. The graph shows the displacement s of a model train moving along
    a track in time t.

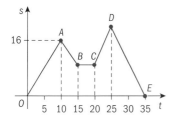

    The velocity of the train from O to A is $V\,\mathrm{m\,s^{-1}}$ and from A to B the velocity
    is $-V\,\mathrm{m\,s^{-1}}$. The train is at rest between B and C, and between C and D
    the velocity is $1.5V\,\mathrm{m\,s^{-1}}$. Calculate

    a) the value of V
    b) the displacement from A to B
    c) the displacement from C to D
    d) the displacement from D to E
    e) the velocity between D and E.

Did you know?
The examples in Section 1.1 are a simplification of what
happens in real-life. In practice, although a particle
(or body) can travel at a constant velocity, change in
velocity is never instantaneous. It involves **acceleration**
or **deceleration**.

Imagine sitting in a car where the
velocity changed abruptly. What would happen to
your body if it sped up, slowed down, stopped,
or changed direction in no time at all?

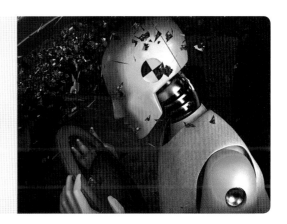

1.2 Velocity–time graphs

A **velocity–time graph** is also used to show the motion of a particle in one dimension, along a straight line. In the next set of examples, motion follows one or more stages of constant velocity or constant acceleration, with the particle moving forwards and backwards along the straight line. In velocity–time graphs, time (t) is shown on the horizontal axis. Velocity is denoted by v.

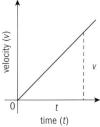

We know that acceleration = $\dfrac{\text{velocity}}{\text{time}}$, which can be abbreviated as acceleration = $\dfrac{v}{t}$.

> Acceleration is the gradient of the velocity–time graph.

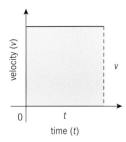

When velocity is constant, displacement = velocity × time, or more simply, $v \times t$. Therefore,

> For constant velocity, displacement is found by calculating the area of the rectangle on a velocity–time graph.

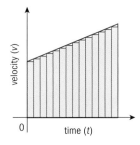

When acceleration is constant, the velocity graph will be a straight line. Consider the area under the graph to be made of a series of very narrow rectangles. The area of each of these rectangles is the displacement of the particle over a very short time. Combining these areas, we get an approximation for the area of the trapezium under the graph, which improves as the time period for each rectangle becomes less.

> Displacement is the area under the velocity–time graph.

Example 2

During the first 10 s of a journey along a straight road, a car accelerates from rest to a velocity of 20 m s^{-1}. It then continues for a further 20 s at constant velocity.

a) Sketch the velocity–time graph of the journey.

b) Calculate the acceleration during the first 10 s of the journey.

c) Describe the motion between the first 10 s and 30 s of the journey.

d) Calculate the total distance travelled in the first 30 s of the journey.

a)

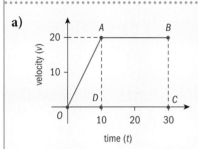

b) Since acceleration = $\dfrac{\text{velocity}}{\text{time}}$, the gradient of a velocity–time graph is the acceleration.

The gradient of OA is $\dfrac{20}{10} = 2$.

The acceleration in the first 10 s is 2 m s^{-2}.

c) The gradient of the graph is 0 between A and B. Therefore, the acceleration is 0 m s^{-2}. This is constant velocity.

d) Since displacement = velocity × time, the displacement is found by calculating the area under the graph between $t = 0$ and $t = 30$.

Total area = area of OAD + area of $ABCD$

$$= \frac{1}{2} \times 10 \times 20 + 20 \times 20$$

$$= 500$$

Note: Velocity away from O is regarded as positive. Lines with a positive gradient show positive acceleration and those with a negative slope show negative acceleration (deceleration).

or

Total area = area of trapezium $OABC$

$$= \frac{1}{2}(30 + 20) \times 20$$

$$= 500$$

Hint: Using the trapezium formula is often quicker and more straightforward than breaking the area into simpler shapes.

The displacement in the first 30 s is 500 m.

In a velocity–time graph, velocity can be positive (above the time axis) or negative (below the time axis). Performing calculations from values in the graph can result in areas that are negative as well, indicating a negative displacement. Care needs to be taken when finding displacement if both positive and negative velocities are involved.

Consider the case of a cricket ball thrown up in the air. There is a positive displacement as the ball travels up, and a negative displacement as it travels back down. Since the ball returns to the point where it started, the overall displacement is zero. The distance travelled, however, is not equal to zero. The difference between displacement (a **vector** quantity) and distance (a **scalar** quantity) will be discussed in Chapter 2.

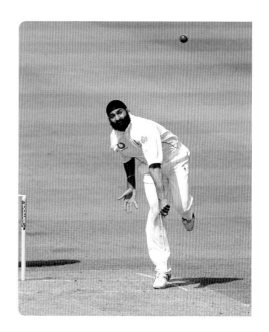

Example 3

A ball is projected up a **smooth** plane at a velocity of $15\,\mathrm{m\,s^{-1}}$ from a point O. The ball decelerates at a constant rate for $6\,\mathrm{s}$. The ball is instantaneously at rest at $t = 3\,\mathrm{s}$.

a) Sketch the velocity–time graph for the ball's journey.

b) Calculate the value of the ball's acceleration.

c) What is the maximum displacement of the ball?

d) What is the total distance travelled by the ball?

- -

a)

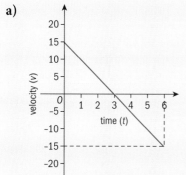

b) Gradient $= \dfrac{-30}{6} = \dfrac{-15}{3} = -5$

The acceleration is $-5\,\mathrm{m\,s^{-2}}$.

c) The maximum displacement of the ball occurs when it is at rest, when $t = 3\,\mathrm{s}$.

Area $= \dfrac{1}{2} \times 3 \times 15 = 22.5$

The maximum displacement is $22.5\,\mathrm{m}$.

d) Between $t = 3$ and $t = 6$, the displacement is $-22.5\,\mathrm{m}$, and hence the total displacement of the ball is $22.5 + (-22.5) = 0\,\mathrm{m}$. This simply means that the ball has returned to its starting position.

The total *distance* travelled is $2 \times 22.5 = 45\,\mathrm{m}$.

Another difference between vector and scalar quantities is that between velocity and speed. Consider two cars that hit each other on a highway travelling at the same velocity, and two other cars that hit each other head-on at the same speed.

- **Result**: the first two cars have only minor damage, while the second two have significant damage.

What is a possible explanation for this difference in damage?

- **The reason**: two cars travelling at the same velocity are travelling in the same direction, and so they hit each other in a side-on collision, causing less damage. In straight-line motion, speed could be in opposite directions, and a head-on collision would cause much more damage.

Example 4

A car accelerates smoothly from rest for 30 s to a velocity of $20\,\mathrm{m\,s^{-1}}$. It continues at a steady velocity for 20 s before decelerating to rest in 20 s.

a) Sketch the velocity–time graph of the motion of the car in the first 70 s of motion.

b) Calculate the acceleration in the first 30 s and the final 20 s.

c) Calculate the total displacement.

d) Calculate the average speed during the journey.

· ·

a)

velocity (v) vs time (t) graph: velocity rises linearly from 0 at t=0 to 20 at t=30, stays constant at 20 until t=50, then decreases linearly to 0 at t=70. Axes marked 10, 20 on velocity; 10, 20, 30, 40, 50, 60, 70, 80 on time.

b) Since acceleration $= \dfrac{\text{velocity}}{\text{time}}$, the gradient of a velocity–time graph is the acceleration.

The gradient in the first 30 s is $\dfrac{20}{30} = \dfrac{2}{3} \approx 0.667$.

The acceleration in the first 30 s is $0.667\,\mathrm{m\,s^{-2}}$.

The gradient in the last 20 s is $\dfrac{-20}{20} = -1$.

The acceleration in the last 20 s is $-1\,\mathrm{m\,s^{-2}}$.

▶ Continued on the next page

c) Since displacement = velocity × time, the displacement is found by calculating the area under the graph between $t = 0$ and $t = 70$.

Total area = area of trapezium

$$= \frac{1}{2}(70 + 20) \times 20$$

$$= 900$$

The total displacement is 900 m.

d) Average speed = $\dfrac{\text{total displacement}}{\text{time taken}}$

$$= \frac{900}{70} \approx 12.9\,\text{m s}^{-1}$$

 Examination advice

It is a common error not to use the correct formula when calculating average speed. Make sure that you learn this formula:

average speed = $\dfrac{\text{total displacement}}{\text{time taken}}$

Note: Average speed is *not* found by taking the average of two speeds.

Exercise 1.2

1. A car is travelling at $30\,\text{m s}^{-1}$. It continues at a constant velocity for 20 s, and then slows to a halt after a further 10 s. Sketch a velocity–time graph to show the motion of the car.

2. A baseball is thrown vertically upwards from the ground with an initial velocity of $20\,\text{m s}^{-1}$. The acceleration due to gravity is $10\,\text{m s}^{-2}$ downwards. Sketch a velocity–time graph to show the motion of the baseball from the time it is thrown until it reaches the ground again.

3. A train leaves a station and accelerates uniformly for 10 s until it reaches a velocity of $24\,\text{m s}^{-1}$. It then travels at a constant velocity for 60 s until it approaches the next station when it decelerates uniformly at a rate of $2\,\text{m s}^{-2}$. Sketch a velocity–time graph to show the motion of the train.

   Note: In the graphs that follow, velocity (v) is given in metres per second and time (t) in seconds.

4.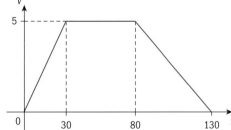

   The velocity–time graph shows the motion of boat moving along a straight canal. The boat moves forward for 30 s, accelerating from rest to a velocity of $5\,\text{m s}^{-1}$, then moves for another 50 s at a constant velocity and finally decelerates for another 50 s until it is at rest again. Calculate

   a) the acceleration when $t = 10$ and $t = 100$

   b) the total distance covered

   c) the average speed for the whole journey.

5. The velocity–time graph shows the first 35 s of the motion of a car as it moves onto a highway. In the first 10 s it accelerates from rest to $16 \, \text{m s}^{-1}$ on the slip road. It then travels for 10 s on the slip road at a constant velocity before joining the highway and accelerating for another 15 s to reach a velocity of $40 \, \text{m s}^{-1}$. Find

    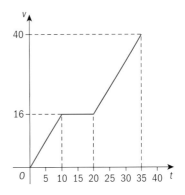

    a) the acceleration when $t = 5$ and $t = 30$

    b) the distance travelled by the car on the slip road

    c) the total distance travelled by the car during the first 35 s.

6.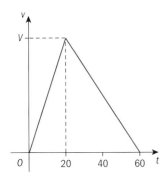

    A particle accelerates to a velocity V in 20 s and then decelerates back to rest in 40 s. Find

    a) V if the total distance travelled is 450 m

    b) the acceleration in the first 20 s

    c) the total distance travelled in the first 40 s.

7.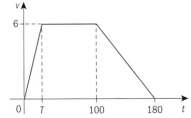

    In a mineshaft, an elevator is bringing coal from a coal mine below ground. The motion of the elevator is modelled by three straight-line segments. The first is acceleration from rest to $6 \, \text{m s}^{-1}$, the second is motion at a uniform velocity and the third is deceleration back to rest. Find

    a) T, the time that it takes to accelerate if the initial acceleration is $0.2 \, \text{m s}^{-2}$

    b) the total distance travelled by the elevator

    c) the average speed of the elevator.

8.

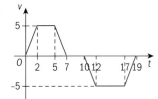

The velocity–time graph shows the motion of an elevator travelling in a building. There are seven stages in its journey. It accelerates from rest to $5\,\mathrm{m\,s^{-1}}$, and then travels at a constant velocity before decelerating back to rest. It remains stationary before moving downwards, again accelerating, moving with constant velocity and decelerating. The times taken for each of these stages are shown on the graph. Calculate

a) the acceleration for each stage of the journey

b) the distance travelled moving upwards

c) the distance travelled moving downwards

d) If each floor in the building measures 2.5 m and the elevator starts on the 8th floor, on which floor does it first stop, and on which floor is it when it stops after 19 seconds?

9.

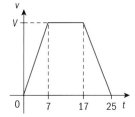

Use the graph. Given that the total displacement is 420 m, find

a) the value of V

b) the acceleration at time $t = 5$

c) the acceleration at time $t = 20$

d) the times at which the speed is $6\,\mathrm{m\,s^{-1}}$.

10. Use the graph. If the total displacement is 380 m, find

a) the value of V

b) the value of the deceleration when $t = 8$ and $t = 30$

c) the average speed for the whole journey.

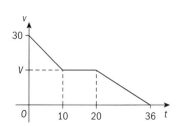

11.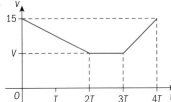

Use the graph. Given that the total distance travelled is 70 m and that the initial deceleration is 2.5 m s^{-2}, find

a) the possible values of V

b) the possible values of T.

12.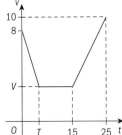

Use the graph. If the total displacement is 138 m and the initial deceleration is 1 m s^{-2}, find

a) the value of V

b) the value of T.

13. A ball is thrown upwards at a speed of 20 m s^{-1} from a tower that is 25 m high. It goes up into the air and then falls all the way to the ground without hitting the tower. When it reaches the ground, it bounces back up at half the speed it hit the ground with. It comes to rest when it hits the ground for the second time. Times are shown on the velocity–time graph. If the acceleration due to gravity is –10 m s^{-2}, find

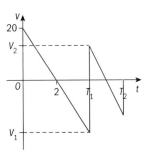

a) the greatest height it reaches above the ground

b) the time it takes to reach the ground

c) its velocity V_1 when it first hits the ground

d) its velocity V_2 when it rebounds

e) the greatest height it reaches above the ground after it bounces

f) the total time T taken for the ball to come to rest.

Summary exercise 1

1. In a game of pool, a ball is directly hit towards the cushion at a speed of $10\,\mathrm{m\,s^{-1}}$. When it hits the cushion, it changes direction, returning at a speed of $8\,\mathrm{m\,s^{-1}}$. It takes $0.04\,\mathrm{s}$ for the ball to reach the cushion.

   a) Find the distance that the ball travels between the starting point and the cushion.

   b) Sketch a displacement–time graph showing the motion of the ball until the time that it returns to its starting position.

EXAM-STYLE QUESTION

2. Two stations at A and B are on a section of straight track and are $800\,\mathrm{m}$ apart. A train passes through A at $t = 0$ at a constant speed of $20\,\mathrm{m\,s^{-1}}$ in the direction of B. A second train passes through B at $t = 5$ at a speed of $20\,\mathrm{m\,s^{-1}}$ in the opposite direction towards A. After a further $10\,\mathrm{s}$, the second train increases its speed to $25\,\mathrm{m\,s^{-1}}$ in the same direction.

   a) Sketch, on the same diagram, a displacement–time graph to model the motion of the two trains.

   b) Where and at what time do the two trains pass each other?

   c) Which train passes through the station at the opposite end of the track first?

3.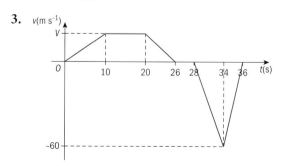

A roller coaster in an amusement park is known as 'The Long Drop'. The ride takes just over half a minute from beginning to end. The car starts at ground level and is carried upwards from rest. It accelerates uniformly and then travels for $10\,\mathrm{s}$ at constant velocity before decelerating and coming to a stop at the top of the track. Here it waits for $2\,\mathrm{s}$ before dropping back to the ground. After dropping for $6\,\mathrm{s}$ it decelerates rapidly for a further $2\,\mathrm{s}$, coming to a halt at ground level. It reaches a maximum speed of $30\,\mathrm{m\,s^{-1}}$ on its descent. Calculate

   a) the distance that the car falls on its descent

   b) the maximum velocity V that it reaches on its ascent

   c) the value of the deceleration in the final phase before the car comes to a halt

   d) the distance that the car drops before it begins to decelerate.

EXAM-STYLE QUESTION

4.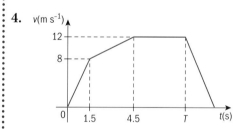

A $100\,\mathrm{m}$ sprinter accelerates to $8\,\mathrm{m\,s^{-1}}$ in $1.5\,\mathrm{s}$. He then accelerates to $12\,\mathrm{m\,s^{-1}}$ in the next $3\,\mathrm{s}$ and runs at a constant speed for the remainder of the race. He completes the race in $T\,\mathrm{s}$. After he passes the finish, he decelerates and stops further along the track. Find

   a) the time he takes to complete the race

   b) his deceleration at the end of the race if he runs a further $20\,\mathrm{m}$ before coming to a stop.

5. A particle decelerates from a speed of $40\,\mathrm{m\,s^{-1}}$ to a speed V in 10 s. It travels at speed V for a further 10 s and then decelerates to rest in 16 s. The initial deceleration is $2\,\mathrm{m\,s^{-2}}$.

   a) Sketch a velocity–time graph for the particle.

   b) Find the value of V.

   c) Find the average velocity for the whole journey.

6. A particle decelerates from an initial velocity of $12\,\mathrm{m\,s^{-1}}$ to a velocity V in T s. It continues at speed V until 15 s after it started. It then accelerates again so that 25 s after the particle started its velocity is $20\,\mathrm{m\,s^{-1}}$. The final acceleration is $1.8\,\mathrm{m\,s^{-2}}$. The particle travels a total distance of 179 m.

   a) Sketch a velocity–time graph for the particle.

   b) Calculate the value of V.

   c) Calculate the value of T.

Chapter summary

Displacement–time graph

- A displacement–time graph is used to show the motion of a particle, in one dimension, along a straight line.
- Velocity = gradient of displacement–time graph
- Displacement is often denoted by s.

Velocity–time graph

- A velocity–time graph is also used to show the motion of a particle in one dimension, along a straight line.
- Acceleration = gradient of velocity–time graph
- Displacement = area under velocity–time graph
  - For constant velocity, displacement is found by calculating the area of the rectangle on a velocity–time graph.
- Average speed $= \dfrac{\text{total displacement}}{\text{time taken}}$

Note: It is a common error to use the incorrect formula for average speed, so make sure to learn this formula.

Sprinters at the start of a race increase their speed at a constant rate. They are accelerating uniformly for the first few seconds of the race until they reach top speed. In the 100 m race, the track is a straight line, and sprinters typically reach their top speed after 50–60 m. There are many situations in which the acceleration formulae we are about to study can be used to model motion in a straight line with constant (uniform) acceleration. For example, the acceleration due to gravity is constant, and these formulae are used in a huge number of situations involving falling bodies.

Objectives

- Understand the concepts of distance and speed as scalar quantities, and of displacement, velocity and acceleration as vector quantities.
- Use appropriate formulae for motion with constant acceleration in a straight line.

Before you start

You should know how to:

1. Substitute values into a formula.

e.g. If $a = 3$, $b = 4$ and $c = -5$, then the value of $u = a^2 + 2bc$ is

$u = 3^2 + 2 \times 4 \times (-5) = -31$

2. Solve linear equations.

e.g. Solve $8 = -2 + 4t$:

$8 + 2 = 4t$

$\quad 10 = 4t$

$\quad\quad t = 2.5$

3. Solve quadratic equations by factorising or using the quadratic formula.

e.g. Solve the following quadratic equations for t.

a) $t^2 - 7t + 10 = 0$

Factorise the quadratic to get

$(t - 2)(t - 5) = 0$, giving $t = 2$ or $t = 5$.

Skills check:

1. Given that $a = 3$, $b = 4$ and $c = -2$, evaluate

a) $2a^2 - b$ **b)** $a(b - c)$ **c)** $\dfrac{b^2 - c^2}{2a}$

2. Solve these linear equations:

a) $2u + 7 = 15$

b) $9 - 3a = 1$

c) $4t - 11 = -5$

3. Solve these quadratic equations, giving answers to 3 s.f. where appropriate.

a) $t^2 - 8t + 12 = 0$

b) $2t^2 - 3t - 1 = 0$

c) $3t^2 + 2t = 4$

b) $t^2 + 2t - 6 = 0$

Use the quadratic formula

$t = \dfrac{-b \pm \sqrt{b^2 - 4ac}}{2a}$ to get

$t = \dfrac{-2 \pm \sqrt{2^2 - 4 \times 1 \times (-6)}}{2 \times 1}$, giving

$t = 1.65$ (3 s.f.) or $t = -3.65$ (3 s.f.)

2.1 Constant-acceleration formulae

When the motion of a body is being considered, the conventional variables that we use are

s = displacement

u = initial velocity

v = final velocity

a = acceleration

t = time.

When working with variables such as these, it is important to make the distinction between scalar and vector quantities:

- Scalar quantities have magnitude (size) only.
- Vector quantities have magnitude as well as direction.

Excluding time, the characteristics of motion are vector quantities, where the direction is equally as important as the magnitude.

- **Displacement** is a vector quantity, which gives the position of a body relative to an origin.
- **Distance** is a scalar quantity, which states how far the body has travelled.
- **Velocity** is a vector quantity, which tells us how fast the body is moving and in what direction.
- **Speed** is a scalar quantity, which tells us how fast the body is moving only. It is the magnitude of the velocity.

In Chapter 1, a number of relationships were seen between variables. You looked at graphs that represented the displacement, velocities and acceleration of bodies in motion. There are several simple formulae we use when dealing with constant acceleration.

Consider the velocity–time graph opposite, showing the motion of a body with initial velocity u and final velocity v after t seconds have elapsed.

The gradient of the line is calculated from the expression

$$\frac{v-u}{t}$$

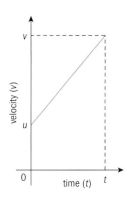

Since the gradient of this line is equal to the value of the acceleration, a, then

$$a = \frac{v-u}{t}$$

This can be rewritten to make v the subject, as

$$v = u + at \tag{1}$$

This formula can be used in problems where three of the four quantities are known. However this is not always the case. Consider the area of the trapezium under the velocity–time graph. We know from Chapter 1 that this area is equal to the displacement, s, of the body, and so we obtain the formula

$$s = \frac{1}{2}(u + v)t \tag{2}$$

From the graph, we have derived two important formulae. If we eliminate v from equations (1) and (2), we obtain

$$s = \frac{1}{2}(u + (u + at))t$$

which simplifies to

$$s = ut + \frac{1}{2}at^2 \tag{3}$$

If we eliminate t from equations (1) and (2), we obtain

$$s = \frac{1}{2}(u+v) \times \frac{v-u}{a}$$

which simplifies and rearranges to

$$v^2 = u^2 + 2as \tag{4}$$

These four formulae, known as the constant-acceleration formulae, can be used to solve problems, provided that we can make the modelling assumption that acceleration is uniform.

Note that when acceleration is not uniform, these formulae are not valid and should not be used. This will be discussed later in the book.

Note: These equations are also commonly referred to as the *suvat* equations.

Example 1

A car travelling at $6\,\mathrm{m\,s^{-1}}$ accelerates at $2\,\mathrm{m\,s^{-2}}$. Calculate its speed 8 seconds later.

s is not required
$u = 6$
$v = \,?$
$a = 2$
$t = 8$

The formula that involves u, v, a, t is $v = u + at$

So $\quad v = 6 + 2 \times 8 = 22\,\mathrm{m\,s^{-1}}$

Example 2

A car, initially travelling at $8\,\mathrm{m\,s^{-1}}$, accelerates at a constant rate of $3\,\mathrm{m\,s^{-2}}$ until it is travelling at $17\,\mathrm{m\,s^{-1}}$. Find

a) the distance travelled while accelerating

b) the time taken to accelerate.

a) $s = \,?$

$u = 8$

$v = 17$

$a = 3$

t is not required

Use $v^2 = u^2 + 2as$: $17^2 = 8^2 + 2 \times 3 \times s$

So $s = 37.5\,\mathrm{m}$

b) s is not required

$u = 8$

$v = 17$

$a = 3$

$t = \,?$

Use $v = u + at$: $17 = 8 + 3 \times t$

So $t = 3\,\mathrm{s}$

Example 3

According to driving guidelines the minimum braking distance for a car travelling at $20\,\text{m s}^{-1}$ is $30\,\text{m}$. Find

a) the deceleration of the car

b) the time it would take for the car to stop.

> **Note:** Braking distance is the distance a car travels from the point where its brakes are applied to the point where it comes to a complete stop.

a) $s = 30$

   $u = 20$

   $v = 0$

   $a = ?$

   t is not required

   Use $v^2 = u^2 + 2as$:

   $0^2 = 20^2 + 2 \times a \times 30$

   So $a = -6\frac{2}{3}\,\text{m s}^{-2}$

   Hence the deceleration is $6\frac{2}{3}\,\text{m s}^{-2}$.

b) $s = 30$

   $u = 20$

   $v = 0$

   a is not required

   $t = ?$

   Use $s = \frac{1}{2}(u + v)t$:

   $30 = \frac{1}{2}(20 + 0)t$

   So $t = 3\,\text{s}$

Example 4

Two points A and B are $8\,\text{m}$ apart and lie in the same horizontal plane. A particle passes point A with a speed of $2\,\text{m s}^{-1}$ in the direction of point B. The particle is accelerating at a constant rate of $4\,\text{m s}^{-2}$ in the direction of its motion. At the same time a second particle is passing point B with a speed of $3\,\text{m s}^{-1}$ in the direction of point A. The second particle is accelerating at a constant rate of $2\,\text{m s}^{-2}$ in the direction of its motion.

Determine the time in seconds that has passed when the particles meet, and their position when this happens.

The formula that involves s, u, a and t is $s = ut + \frac{1}{2}at^2$.

For the first particle, $u = 2$ and $a = 4$.

$s = 2t + \frac{1}{2} \times 4 \times t^2 = 2t + 2t^2$

For the second particle, $u = -3$ and $a = -2$.

$s = 8 + (-3)t + \frac{1}{2} \times (-2)t^2 = 8 - 3t - t^2$

← Find s in terms of t for each particle.

▶ Continued on the next page

At the point where the two particles meet

$$2t+2t^2 = 8-3t-t^2$$

$$3t^2+5t-8=0$$

$$(3t+8)(t-1)=0$$

Solving the quadratic equation for t gives $t=-\dfrac{8}{3}$ or $t=1$.

Since t cannot be negative in this problem, $t=1$ s.

When $t=1$

$$s=2\times1+2\times1^2=4 \text{ m}$$

So the particles meet 4 m from A.

Note: In Examples 1–4, all of the bodies have size, but the modelling assumptions we make are for all bodies to be particles so that air resistance can be ignored.

Exercise 2.1

In questions **1** to **10**, a particle is moving with constant acceleration $a\,\mathrm{m\,s^{-2}}$ along a straight line. The velocity at the point O is $u\,\mathrm{m\,s^{-1}}$, and t seconds later the velocity is $v\,\mathrm{m\,s^{-1}}$. The displacement from O at time t is s metres.

1. Find s when $u = 0$, $a = 4$, $t = 8$.
2. Find s when $u = 3$, $v = 5$, $t = 10$.
3. Find v when $u = 3$, $a = 2$, $t = 6$.
4. Find u when $s = 28$, $a = 1$, $t = 4$.
5. Find a when $s = 500$, $u = 1$, $t = 10$.
6. Find t when $u = 3$, $v = 7$, $a = 0.2$.
7. Find t when $u = 5$, $a = 1$, $s = 12$.
8. Find s when $u = 2$, $v = 10$, $a = 4$.
9. Find u when $s = 50$, $v = 6$, $t = 10$.
10. Find v when $s = 132$, $a = 2$, $t = 12$.

11. A train leaves a station and accelerates uniformly at a rate of $0.4\,\mathrm{m\,s^{-2}}$. The train is in motion for 50 seconds.

    a) Find how far from the station the train is at this time.

    b) Find the speed of the train at this time.

12. A car passes a point O on a straight road with velocity $4\,\mathrm{m\,s^{-1}}$. It accelerates at a constant rate of $2.5\,\mathrm{m\,s^{-2}}$ to a velocity of $9\,\mathrm{m\,s^{-1}}$. It then decelerates at a rate of $2\,\mathrm{m\,s^{-2}}$, reducing its speed to $3\,\mathrm{m\,s^{-1}}$.

    a) Find the distance that the car travels while accelerating. Hence find the total distance travelled by the car.

    b) Find the total time the car takes to travel this distance.

13. A man drives a car with a constant acceleration of $4\,\mathrm{m\,s^{-2}}$. After 2 seconds of accelerating he sees a set of traffic lights and slows down with a deceleration of $1.5\,\mathrm{m\,s^{-2}}$. Given that the initial velocity of the car is $1\,\mathrm{m\,s^{-1}}$ and the car stops at the traffic lights, find the distance between the traffic lights and the point where he starts to accelerate.

14. An elevator ascends from rest with an acceleration of $0.6\,\mathrm{m\,s^{-2}}$, before slowing down with a deceleration of $0.8\,\mathrm{m\,s^{-2}}$ for the next stop. The total time taken is 10 seconds. Find the distance between the stops.

15. a) A particle moves along a straight line AB with a constant acceleration $0.5\,\mathrm{m\,s^{-2}}$. If the distance AB is $15\,\mathrm{m}$ and it takes 3 seconds to travel from A to B, find the velocity of the particle at A.

    b) A second particle is projected along a line parallel to AB at the same time with a constant acceleration of $1.5\,\mathrm{m\,s^{-2}}$. If the second particle also takes $3\,\mathrm{s}$ to travel a distance of $15\,\mathrm{m}$, determine the initial velocity of the second particle.

2.2 Vertical motion

It was the work of **Sir Isaac Newton (1642–1727)** that made us realise that objects in free fall accelerated towards the ground at a constant rate.

The constant acceleration formulae developed in Section 2.1 may be used when considering the motion of bodies falling under gravity. In such cases, the acceleration of the body is widely used as $9.8\,\mathrm{m\,s^{-2}}$, but often when you are set a question, it will state that an approximation of $10\,\mathrm{m\,s^{-2}}$ is to be used. This value is usually referred to as g, the acceleration due to gravity.

Q **Examination advice**
Questions in Cambridge examinations will always expect use of $g = 10\,\mathrm{m\,s^{-2}}$.

Sign convention

When working through any example, care is needed to ensure that the directions of vectors involved are consistent. One way of doing this is to adopt a sign convention, where the positive direction is designated before assigning values to the *suvat* variables.

Example 5

A ball is thrown vertically downwards from the top of a building at a speed of $2.5\,\mathrm{m\,s^{-1}}$. If the height of the building is $20\,\mathrm{m}$, find

a) the speed with which the ball hits the ground

b) the time taken for the ball to reach the ground.

▶ Continued on the next page

---

a) If we adopt the convention that positive is downwards for this question, then

$s = 20$

$u = 2.5$

$v = ?$

$a = g = 10$

t is not required

Use $v^2 = u^2 + 2as$:

$v^2 = 2.5^2 + 2 \times 10 \times 20$

So $v = 20.15564437 \approx 20.2\,\mathrm{m\,s}^{-1}$ (3 s.f.)

b) $s = 20$

$u = 2.5$

$v = 20.15564437$

$a = g = 10$

$t = ?$

Use $v = u + at$:

$20.15564437 = 2.5 + 10t$

So $t = 1.76554437 \approx 1.77\,\mathrm{s}$ (3 s.f.)

Note: The final answers are rounded to 3 s.f. But do not use rounded answers in another calculation.

Example 6

A ball is thrown vertically upwards from ground level at a speed of $15\,\mathrm{m\,s}^{-1}$. Find

a) the greatest height reached by the ball

b) the time taken for the ball to return to ground level.

a) If we adopt the convention that positive is upwards for this question, then

$s = ?$

$u = 15$

$v = 0$

$a = -g = -10$

t is not required

Use $v^2 = u^2 + 2as$:

$0^2 = 15^2 + 2 \times (-10) \times s$

So $s = 11.25\,\mathrm{m}$

b) $s = 0$

$u = 15$

v is not required

$a = -g = -10$

$t = ?$

Use $s = ut + \dfrac{1}{2}at^2$:

$0 = 15t + \dfrac{1}{2} \times (-10) \times t^2$

So $t = 0\,\mathrm{s}$ or $t = 3\,\mathrm{s}$

Hence, the time taken to return to ground level is 3 seconds.

Examination advice

Note that in Examples 5 and 6, we use the modelling assumption of ignoring air resistance, so that the acceleration is then constant and equal to the acceleration due to gravity. This also means that the motion in Example 6 is symmetric. So, for part (b), we could have worked out the time to the highest point (1.5 seconds) from using $v = u + at$, which is the same as the time from the highest point back to ground level, hence the time required is double the time to the highest point. You can use this method to solve questions of the same type as in Examples 5 and 6.

Exercise 2.2

In this exercise, take g as $10\,\mathrm{m\,s^{-2}}$ and give answers correct to 3 significant figures where appropriate.

1. A book falls from a shelf $1.8\,\mathrm{m}$ above the floor.

   Find the speed with which the book strikes the floor.

2. A stone is dropped from $48\,\mathrm{m}$ above the ground.
   Find the time it takes for the stone to reach the ground.

3. A stone is dropped from the top of a cliff and falls to ground level.
   If the stone hits the ground at $18\,\mathrm{m\,s^{-1}}$, find the height of the cliff.

4. A ball is thrown vertically upwards at a speed of $25\,\mathrm{m\,s^{-1}}$ and travels freely under gravity. Find the velocity of the ball after 2 seconds, and the distance the ball has travelled from the start at this time.

5. For the ball in question **4**, find the maximum height reached by the ball, and the total time taken to return to its starting position.

6. A stone is thrown vertically upwards at a speed of $12\,\mathrm{m\,s^{-1}}$, from $5\,\mathrm{m}$ above horizontal ground. Find

   a) the speed with which the stone hits the ground

   b) the time taken for the stone to hit the ground.

7. A ball is dropped from a height of $30\,\mathrm{m}$. Find

   a) the time taken for the ball to reach the ground

   b) the speed at which the ball hits the ground.

8. A ball is thrown vertically upwards with an initial speed of $8\,\mathrm{m\,s^{-1}}$ from a height of $1\,\mathrm{m}$ above level ground. Find

   a) the time when the speed of the ball is zero

   b) the greatest height above the ground reached by the ball

   c) the speed of the ball when it hits the ground.

9. A boy drops a ball from rest from the top of a building. At the same time, his friend throws a ball vertically upwards from the base of the building at a speed of $30\,\mathrm{m\,s^{-1}}$. The two balls collide after $1.8\,\mathrm{s}$. Find the distance from the ground to the top of the building.

10. A ball is thrown vertically upwards from a point O at a speed of $30\,\mathrm{m\,s^{-1}}$.

    a) Find the time that the ball is a height of $25\,\mathrm{m}$ above point O

      i) for the first time

      ii) for the second time.

    b) Find the total time that the height of the ball above point O is at least $25\,\mathrm{m}$.

11. A particle is projected vertically upwards from a fixed point O. The speed of projection is $u\,\mathrm{m\,s^{-1}}$. The particle returns to O 4 seconds later. Find

  a) the value of u

  b) the greatest height reached by the particle

  c) the total time for which the particle is at a height greater than half its greatest height.

12. An object is projected vertically upwards at a speed of $9\,\mathrm{m\,s^{-1}}$. Calculate

  a) the speed of the object when it is $2.4\,\mathrm{m}$ above the point of projection

  b) the greatest height of the object above the point of projection

  c) the time after projection when the object is travelling downwards at a speed of $4.6\,\mathrm{m\,s^{-1}}$.

13. At the same time, particle P is projected vertically upwards from horizontal ground at a speed of $8\,\mathrm{m\,s^{-1}}$.

  a) Show that the greatest height above ground reached by P is $3.2\,\mathrm{m}$.

  A particle Q is projected vertically from a point $1.4\,\mathrm{m}$ above the ground at a speed of $u\,\mathrm{m\,s^{-1}}$. The greatest height above the ground reached by Q is also $3.2\,\mathrm{m}$.

  b) Find the value of u.

  c) Find the speed and direction of both particles when P and Q are at the same height.

Summary exercise 2

1. A ball is dropped onto level ground from a height of $20\,\mathrm{m}$.

  a) Calculate the time taken for the ball to reach the ground.

  The ball rebounds (bounces back) with half the speed it strikes the ground.

  b) Calculate the time taken for the ball to reach the ground a second time after the initial bounce.

2. A rocket is travelling with a velocity of $80\,\mathrm{m\,s^{-1}}$. The engines are switched on for 8 seconds and the rocket accelerates uniformly at $30\,\mathrm{m\,s^{-2}}$.

  a) Calculate the speed of the rocket immediately after the engines are turned off.

  b) Calculate the distance travelled by the rocket while accelerating.

3. A top sprinter in the $100\,\mathrm{m}$ race will accelerate at a rate of $5.5\,\mathrm{m\,s^{-2}}$ in the first 2 seconds of the race.

  a) Find how far the sprinter runs while accelerating.

  b) Assuming that the sprinter runs the rest of the race at the speed he attained after 2 seconds, find the total time he takes to run the race.

4. A ball is thrown vertically upwards from the top of a cliff, which is $80\,\mathrm{m}$ high. The initial speed of the ball is $25\,\mathrm{m\,s^{-1}}$. Find the time taken to reach the bottom of the cliff and the speed of the ball at that instant.

5. A ball is thrown vertically upwards at a speed of $45\,\mathrm{m\,s^{-1}}$. Find the length of time for which the ball is at least $25\,\mathrm{m}$ above the point of release.

6. A car and a lorry are initially at rest side by side. The lorry moves off at a uniform acceleration of $0.6\,\mathrm{m\,s^{-2}}$. After 10 seconds, the car moves off at a uniform acceleration of $1.6\,\mathrm{m\,s^{-2}}$. Find how long the lorry has been in motion when it is overtaken by the car, and find the distance travelled by the lorry in that time.

7. A car starts at rest from a point A and moves in a straight line with uniform acceleration of $1.2\,\mathrm{m\,s^{-2}}$. The car then decelerates at a uniform rate of $1.6\,\mathrm{m\,s^{-1}}$, coming to a stop at B. The total distance covered between A and B is $1600\,\mathrm{m}$. Find the total time for the journey, and the greatest speed attained by the car.

8. A particle moves with a constant acceleration of $0.4\,\mathrm{m\,s^{-2}}$ along a straight line passing through points A and B. It passes point B with a speed $0.8\,\mathrm{m\,s^{-1}}$ greater than its speed at A.

   a) Given that the distance AB is $20\,\mathrm{m}$, calculate the speed at which the particle passes point A.

   b) Find the time after passing A that the particle has a speed of $15\,\mathrm{m\,s^{-1}}$.

9. A particle is projected vertically upwards from a fixed point O. The speed of projection is $5.6\,\mathrm{m\,s^{-1}}$. At time T seconds after projection the particle is at a height of $0.92\,\mathrm{m}$ above O. Find

   a) the two possible values of T

   b) the total time for which the particle is $0.92\,\mathrm{m}$ above O

   c) the height of the particle, above O, when its speed is $2.8\,\mathrm{m\,s^{-1}}$.

Chapter summary

Constant-acceleration formulae

- **Displacement** is a vector quantity, which gives the position of a body relative to an origin.
- **Distance** is a scalar quantity, which states how far the body has travelled.
- **Velocity** is a vector quantity, which tells us how fast the body is moving and in what direction.
- **Speed** is a scalar quantity, which tells us only how fast the body is moving. It is the magnitude of the velocity.

- $v = u + at$
- $s = ut + \dfrac{1}{2}at^2$
- $s = \dfrac{1}{2}(u + v)t$
- $v^2 = u^2 + 2as$

Note: These are known as the *suvat* equations.

Vertical motion

- The acceleration due to gravity (g) acts on bodies falling vertically.
- The value of g is $9.8\,\mathrm{m\,s^{-2}}$, but questions in Cambridge examinations will always use $g = 10\,\mathrm{m\,s^{-2}}$.

Modelling conditions

- All bodies are considered to be particles.
- Air resistance is ignored.

3 Variable acceleration

In the 19th century, Lord Kelvin proposed an analogue machine that would mechanically perform the processes of integration. Vannevar Bush built the first successful machine in 1930 in America, and in 1935, Douglas Hartree built the differential analyser at Manchester University. Hartree's machine was able to perform the calculations required for a number of purposes. During the Second World War, for example, British scientists were able to calculate the trajectories of V2 rockets with it. These analogue machines were the forerunners of modern digital computers that can tackle these calculations with ease.

Objectives
- Use differentiation and integration with respect to time to solve simple problems concerning displacement, velocity and acceleration.

Before you start

You should know how to:

1. Differentiate polynomial functions in x^n (for any rational n).

   e.g.
   $$\frac{d}{dx}\left(3x^2 - \frac{4}{x} + 6x^{\frac{1}{2}}\right) = 6x + \frac{4}{x^2} + 3x^{-\frac{1}{2}}$$

2. Locate stationary points.

   e.g. Find the stationary points of the curve $y = 2x^3 + 3x^2 - 36x + 4$

   $\dfrac{dy}{dx} = 6x^2 + 6x - 36$, so at the stationary points

   $6x^2 + 6x - 36 = 0$

   $x^2 + x - 6 = 0$

   $(x + 3)(x - 2) = 0$

   $x = -3$ or $x = 2$

   Hence the stationary points are $(-3, 85)$ and $(2, -40)$.

Skills check:

1. Differentiate these with respect to x.

   a) $x^2 - 2x$ **b)** $\dfrac{1}{x} - \dfrac{1}{x^2}$ **c)** $\sqrt{x}$

2. Find the maximum and minimum points of the function $y = 9x^2 - 4x^3$.

3. Integrate $(ax + b)^n$ (for any rational n except -1).

   e.g. $\int (2x + 1)^{\frac{1}{2}} \, dx = \frac{2}{3}(2x + 1)^{\frac{3}{2}} \left(\frac{1}{2}\right) + c$

   $\qquad = \frac{1}{3}(2x + 1)^{\frac{3}{2}} + c$

3. Integrate these with respect to x.

   a) $3x^2 + 4x$ b) $\dfrac{1}{2x^2}$ c) $\sqrt{x}$

   d) $(1 + 2x)^3$ e) $\sqrt{2x - 1}$

4. Solve problems involving evaluating a constant of integration.

   e.g. If $\dfrac{dy}{dx} = 3x^2 - 4x$ and $y = 3$ when $x = 1$,

   $y = \int 3x^2 - 4x \, dx$

   $y = x^3 - 2x^2 + c$

   $3 = 1 - 2 + c$

   $c = 4$

   $y = x^3 - 2x^2 + 4$

4. Integrate $2x^2 - x - 1$ with respect to x.
   If the value of the integral is -1 when $x = 1$, find the value of the constant of integration.

5. Evaluate definite integrals.

   e.g. $\int_4^9 3x^{\frac{1}{2}} dx = \left[2x^{\frac{3}{2}} \right]_4^9 = (2 \times 27) - (2 \times 8) = 38$

5. Find $\int_1^2 6x^2 + 2x \, dx$.

3.1 Using differentiation to describe straight-line motion

In Chapters 1 and 2 we looked at straight-line motion where either velocity was constant or acceleration was constant. Constant acceleration occurs when the force applied to an object is constant, as with gravitational force. This is because force is directly proportional to acceleration.

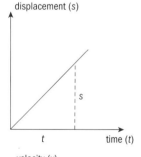

$\text{Velocity} = \dfrac{\text{displacement}}{\text{time}}$, so velocity $= \dfrac{s}{t}$

Velocity = gradient of displacement–time graph

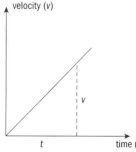

$\text{Acceleration} = \dfrac{\text{velocity}}{\text{time}}$, so acceleration $= \dfrac{v}{t}$

Acceleration = gradient of velocity–time graph

Often in real-life situations, acceleration is neither constant nor does it change suddenly. If you drove out of your garage in the morning and kept accelerating, then you would eventually find yourself travelling beyond the speed limit. If the elevator in your tower block changed suddenly from accelerating upwards to decelerating, you would fall over as a result of the jerk and the lift cable would be likely to break. In reality, the acceleration of objects is changing with time. If we looked at a velocity–time graph the line would be curved and not straight.

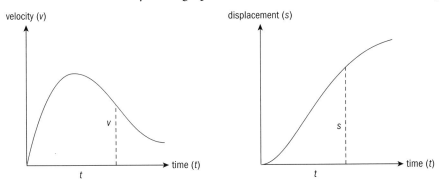

Acceleration is defined as the rate of change of velocity with respect to time. This is the gradient of the curve above. In mathematical terms, we measure the rate at which velocity v changes with respect to time t as the **derivative** $\dfrac{dv}{dt}$. For constant acceleration this is equivalent to our definition of acceleration as the gradient of the velocity–time graph. Similarly, velocity is defined as the rate of change of displacement with respect to time. So the rate at which displacement s changes with respect to time t is $\dfrac{ds}{dt}$.

Note: It is very important to remember that the constant acceleration formulae that you learned in Chapter 2 should only be used where a is a *constant.* Trying to apply these formulae in problems involving variable acceleration will lead to error.

For a particle moving in a straight line: $a = \dfrac{dv}{dt}$ and $v = \dfrac{ds}{dt}$.

Example 1

A car accelerates to overtake a truck on the highway. After passing the truck, the car slows down as it approaches slow-moving traffic, finally coming to a halt. The velocity $v\,\text{m s}^{-1}$ of the car after time t seconds is given by the equation $v = 8 + 0.36t^2 - 0.02t^3$. Find how fast the car is moving when it reaches its maximum velocity.

The acceleration of the car can be found by differentiating v with respect to t:

$$a = \frac{dv}{dt} = 0.72t - 0.06t^2$$

When the car reaches its maximum velocity, the acceleration is momentarily equal to zero.

$$0.72t - 0.06t^2 = 0$$
$$0.06t\,(12 - t) = 0$$
$$t = 0 \text{ or } t = 12$$

The car reaches its maximum velocity after 12 s. To find the velocity, substitute $t = 12$ back into the equation for velocity.

$$v = 8 + 0.36 \times 144 - 0.02 \times 1728$$

$$v = 25.28$$

The maximum velocity is $25.3 \, \mathrm{m \, s^{-1}}$ (3 s.f.).

Example 2

A particle moves on a straight line through O so that its displacement s from O at time t seconds is given by the equation $s = 4 + 12t^2 - t^3$. Find the total distance covered in the first 12 seconds. What will be the acceleration of the particle when it is momentarily at rest?

Distance and displacement are different when in different directions, so we need to check when the particle changes direction. This will occur when $v = 0$.

$$v = \frac{ds}{dt} = 24t - 3t^2 = 3t(8 - t)$$

$$v = 0 \text{ when } t = 0 \text{ or when } t = 8$$

When $t = 6$, $v = 36$ and when $t = 10$, $v = -60$. Since the velocities have opposite signs we can conclude that the particle changes direction in between, when $t = 8$.

When $t = 0$, $s = 4$, when $t = 8$, $s = 260$ and when $t = 12$, $s = 4$.

From this we can see that the total *displacement* between $t = 0$ and $t = 12$ is 0 as the particle returns to the point where it started. The total distance covered is

$$2 \times (260 - 4) = 512 \, \mathrm{m}$$

$$a - \frac{dv}{dt} - 24 - 6t, \text{ so when } t = 8, \, a = 24 - 6 \times 8 = \ -24 \, \mathrm{m \, s^{-2}}$$

Exercise 3.1

1. The velocity of a particle at time t is given by $v = 2t^2 - 4t + 3$. Find the time at which the acceleration is zero.

    Note: Unless otherwise stated, t is in seconds and s is in metres.

2. The velocity of a particle at time t is given by $v = 5 + 4t - 3t^2$. Find the velocity when the acceleration is zero.

3. The velocity v of a particle at time t between $t = 0$ and $t = 3$ is given by $v = t^3 - 6t^2 + 9t$. Find an expression for a and the maximum velocity of the particle.

4. The displacement s of a particle from a point O at time t is given by the equation $s = t(2t - 1)(t + 1)$. Find expressions for the velocity and acceleration of the particle.

5. The displacement s of a particle from a point O at time t is given by the equation $s = 2t^4 - 27t$. Find expressions for the velocity and acceleration of the particle. Find the acceleration at the instant that the velocity is zero.

6. The displacement s of a particle from a point O at time t is given by the equation $s = 2t^3 - 3t^2 - 72$. Find expressions for the velocity and acceleration of the particle. Find the displacement of the particle at the times when it is instantaneously at rest.

7. The velocity v of a particle at time t is given by $v = t^2 + \dfrac{1}{4t}$. Find an expression for the acceleration of the particle. Find the time when the acceleration is zero and the velocity at that instant.

8. The displacement s in metres of a particle from a point O at time t seconds is given by the equation $s = 3\sqrt{t} - \dfrac{1}{2}t$. Find

   a) the time of maximum displacement from O

   b) the time when the velocity of the particle is $0.25\,\mathrm{m\,s^{-1}}$ and the acceleration at that instant.

9. As a train travels from station A to station B, the distance s of the train from station A is modelled by the equation $s = 80t^3 - 60t^4$, where t is measured in hours and s in kilometres. The train first comes to rest at its destination. Find

   a) the time that the journey between the two stations takes

   b) the distance between the two stations

   c) the maximum speed that the train reaches.

10. A particle moves along a straight line though a point O from $t = 0$ until $t = 3$. The displacement s of the particle at time t is given by the equation $s = 2t^3 - 9t^2 + 12t - 4$. Find

a) an expression for the velocity of the particle

b) the times when the particle changes direction

c) the position of the particle at these points

d) the total distance travelled by the particle between $t = 0$ and $t = 3$.

3.2 Using integration to describe straight-line motion

In Section 3.1 we discovered how to find velocity when we know displacement and how to find acceleration when we know velocity. In Chapter 1 we saw that when we wish to find displacement from knowing velocity or find velocity from knowing acceleration then this was done by finding the area under a graph for constant velocity or acceleration.

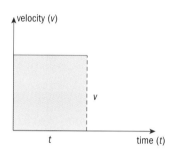

When velocity is constant,

displacement = velocity × time, hence displacement = $v \cdot t$

The displacement is found by calculating the area of the rectangle.

When acceleration is constant, the velocity graph will be a straight line. Consider the area under the graph to be made of a series of very narrow rectangles. The area of each of these rectangles is the displacement in a very short time. Combining these areas, we get an approximation for the area of the trapezium under the graph, which improves as the time period for these rectangles decreases.

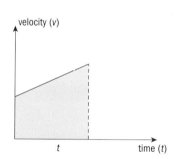

displacement = area under displacement–time graph

In a similar way we found that velocity was the area of a rectangle under an acceleration–time graph when acceleration was constant.

We now look at the situation where acceleration is not constant. As before we will have a curved graph, either a curved velocity–time graph or a curved acceleration–time graph.

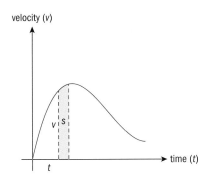

velocity (v)

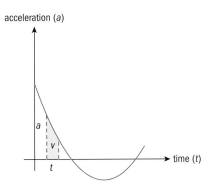

acceleration (a)

Finding the area under a curve is an application of integration (anti-differentiation). We can find displacement when we know velocity and find velocity when we know acceleration by determining **integrals**.

For a particle moving in a straight line:

$$s = \int v\,dt \text{ (an \textbf{indefinite integral}) or } s = \int_{t_1}^{t_2} v\,dt \text{ (a \textbf{definite integral})}$$

$$v = \int a\,dt \text{ (an indefinite integral) or } v = \int_{t_1}^{t_2} a\,dt \text{ (a definite integral)}$$

In the following examples you will see different situations where you will need to use both indefinite integrals (which have a constant of integration in the answer) and definite integrals (evaluated between limits).

Example 3

If the acceleration of a particle that moves along a straight line through a point O at time t is given by the equation $a = 2t^3 - 3t^2$ and the velocity of the particle when $t = 2$ is $10\,\text{m s}^{-1}$, then find an expression for the velocity.

Integrating:

$$v = \int 2t^3 - 3t^2 \, dt$$

$$v = \frac{1}{2}t^4 - t^3 + c$$

When $t = 2$, $v = 8 - 8 + c = 10$

$c = 10$

$$v = \frac{1}{2}t^4 - t^3 + 10$$

In this example we are given a particular value of the displacement function for a given value of time. We use an indefinite integral.

Example 4

If the velocity of a particle that moves along a straight line through O is given by the equation $v = 5t - \frac{1}{2}t^2$, for $0 \le t \le 10$, find the distance travelled between $t = 2$ and $t = 4$.

Integrating between the limits $t = 2$ and $t = 4$:

$$s = \int_2^4 5t - \frac{1}{2}t^2 \, dt$$

$$s = \left[\frac{5}{2}t^2 - \frac{1}{6}t^3 \right]_2^4$$

$$s = \left(40 - \frac{32}{3} \right) - \left(10 - \frac{4}{3} \right)$$

$$s = 20.7 \, \text{m (3 s.f.)}$$

← In this example we do not know the displacement from a fixed point for any value of t. Since we are finding the value between two values of t we use a definite integral.

For a particle moving in a straight line, displacement, velocity and acceleration can be found from each other as summarised in this diagram:

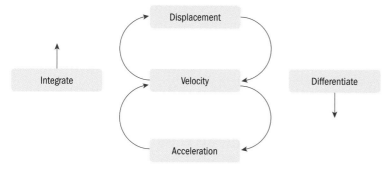

Exercise 3.2

1. The velocity v of a particle at time t is given by $v = 8t^3 - 6t^2 + 5$.
    If the particle starts at a point O, **show that** its displacement from
    O is given by the expression $s = 2t^4 - 2t^3 + 5t$. Unless otherwise stated,
    in this exercise, t is in seconds and s in metres.

2. If the velocity of a particle at time t is given by $v = 15t^4 - 12t^2$ and the
    displacement when $t = 2$ is 34 m, find an expression for the displacement.
    Use this to **determine** the displacement of the particle when $t = 1$.

3. The acceleration of a particle that moves along a straight line through
    a point O is given by $a = 12 - 3t^2$. When $t = 2$, the velocity of the particle
    is 8 m s^{-1} and its displacement from O is 2 m. Find expressions for the
    velocity and displacement of the particle.

4. If the velocity of a particle is given by $v = 20t - 6t^2$, **calculate** the distance
    travelled between $t = 1$ and $t = 3$.

5. A particle moves from rest in a straight line from a point O with acceleration $a = 3t^2 + 4t - 5$. Find its displacement between $t = 1$ and $t = 2$.

6. A car moves away from traffic lights with acceleration $a = 2t - t^2$ and initial velocity $v = 3$. Find an expression for the velocity of the car and its maximum velocity. Use this expression to find the distance travelled before the car reaches its maximum velocity.

7. A particle moves along a straight line through a point O so that its velocity at time t is given by $v = 4(1 + 2t)^3$. Find an expression for its displacement from O, s, given that $s = 2$ when $t = -1$.

8. The acceleration of a particle that moves in a straight line is given by the equation $a = 15\sqrt{2t - 1}$. Find expressions for the velocity v and the displacement s, given that when $t = \frac{1}{2}$, $v = 0$ and $s = 0$.

9. The velocity of a particle that moves along a straight line through O is given by the formula $v = 2t - \frac{2}{t^2}$, $t \geq 1$. Given that $s = 3$ when $t = 1$, find expressions for the displacement of the particle from O and its acceleration.

10. The velocity of a particle that moves along a straight line through O is given by the formula $v = 3t - 2t^2$. When $t = 0$, $s = 0$. Find the maximum velocity and the maximum displacement of the particle from O.

3.3 Deriving the constant-acceleration formulae

At this point it is interesting to see that the constant-acceleration formulae introduced in Chapter 2 are a special case of motion in a straight line, and the equations can be found by using the calculus techniques we have just been learning.

First we should define the parameters and variables we will use.

- a is a constant, equal to the constant acceleration of the particle.
- u is a constant equal to the initial velocity of the particle.
- s is the displacement of the particle from a fixed point O at time t.
- v is the velocity of the particle at time t.

Consider the motion of a particle that starts at point O with an initial velocity u.

$$\frac{dv}{dt} = a$$

$$\int dv = \int a \, dt$$

$$v = at + c_1$$

But when $t = 0$, $v = u$, so $c_1 = u$.

This gives the velocity–time formula $v = u + at$.

$$\frac{ds}{dt} = u + at$$

$$\int ds = \int u + at\ dt$$

$$s = ut + \frac{1}{2}at^2 + c_2$$

But when $t = 0$, $s = 0$, so $c_2 = 0$.

This gives the displacement–time formula

$$s = ut + \frac{1}{2}at^2$$

Other equations can be derived from these by eliminating a or t.

Summary exercise 3

1. A particle starts from rest from a point O and moves in a straight line. Its velocity $v\,\text{m s}^{-1}$ at time t seconds after leaving O is defined as follows.

   For $0 \leq t < 10$, $\quad v = 0.4t - 0.002t^3$

   For $t \geq 10$, $\qquad v = \dfrac{200}{t^2}$

   a) Find the maximum speed of the particle between $t = 0$ and $t = 10$.

   b) Find the total distance travelled in the first 20 s of motion.

2. A car travels in a straight line from A to B starting from rest. The car's speed increases to a maximum and then slows down until it is at rest at B. Its velocity (in m s^{-1}) t seconds after leaving A and until it reaches B is $9.6 \times 10^{-6}(30t^4 - 8t^5)$.

   a) Find the distance AB.

   b) Find the time, after $t = 0$, when the acceleration of the car is zero.

   c) Find the maximum speed of the car.

3. A particle starts from a point O and moves in a straight line until it comes to rest in such a way that its velocity t seconds after leaving O is given by $v = \dfrac{6}{(0.2t + 1)^2} - 1\,\text{m s}^{-1}$.

   a) Find the initial velocity of the particle.

   b) Find the time when it comes to rest.

   c) Find the total distance travelled by the particle.

4. A particle P starts at the point O and travels in a straight line. At time t seconds after leaving O the velocity of P is $v\,\text{m s}^{-1}$, where $v = 0.05t^3 - 0.00125t^4$. Find

   a) the positive value of t for which the acceleration is zero

   b) the distance travelled by P before it changes its direction of motion.

5. Two particles P and Q are travelling along a straight line through a point O. P is decelerating at $1\,\mathrm{m\,s^{-2}}$ and at time $t = 0$, its velocity is $3\,\mathrm{m\,s^{-1}}$ and its displacement from O is $2\,\mathrm{m}$. Q starts from the same point with an initial velocity of $1\,\mathrm{m\,s^{-1}}$ and it is decelerating at a rate of $0.2\,\mathrm{m\,s^{-2}}$. Using calculus techniques, find, when the two particles meet again, how far from O they are and their velocities.

Chapter summary

- For a particle moving in a straight line, displacement, velocity and acceleration can be found from each other as summarised in this diagram:

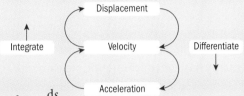

- For a particle moving in a straight line: $a = \dfrac{\mathrm{d}v}{\mathrm{d}t}$ and $v = \dfrac{\mathrm{d}s}{\mathrm{d}t}$.

- For a particle moving in a straight line: $v = \displaystyle\int a\,\mathrm{d}t$ and $s = \displaystyle\int v\,\mathrm{d}t$.

- Between time t_1 and t_2 the change in velocity is found from the *definite* integral $v = \displaystyle\int_{t_1}^{t_2} a\,\mathrm{d}t$ and the displacement is found from the *definite* integral $s = \displaystyle\int_{t_1}^{t_2} v\,\mathrm{d}t$.

Maths in real-life

Challenging technology in sport

Tennis, cricket and soccer are all high-profile sports generating enormous amounts of money at the top level. All have turned to technology based on sophisticated application of some fairly simple mathematical ideas to help improve the decision-making of their officials.

Tennis was the first to adopt the use of 3D computer simulation to predict the path of the ball based on information collected from multiple cameras. The US Open in 2006 was the first Grand Slam event to use it.

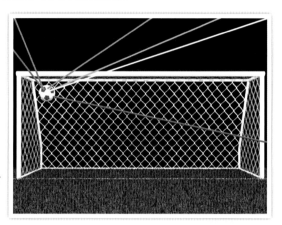

Soccer resisted the use of technology to aid officials' decision-making until July 2012 when the world governing body FIFA approved its use in deciding whether a goal had been scored. The English Premier League implemented its use for the 2013–14 season, and the World Cup in Brazil in 2014 was the first international tournament to use it.

How does it work?

Tennis normally uses 10 highspeed digital cameras that record the position of the ball repeatedly from different angles and heights. These are sent in real time to the central computer running the virtual reality software that uses the 2D images from different cameras to build up a 3D picture of the ball's position at each instant. The sequence of 3D positions is used to generate a trajectory for the ball, which is used to predict its landing position.

▼ The requirements in cricket are much more complex. The first Test match to use it was between New Zealand and Pakistan in 2009.

Is it always used?

No – it is still extremely expensive to install and run, so it is only used at the very top level. The French Open is played on a clay surface, which leaves a mark where the ball lands, so it is not used there. The other tennis Grand Slams use the technology on one or more of the courts on which the most important matches are played.

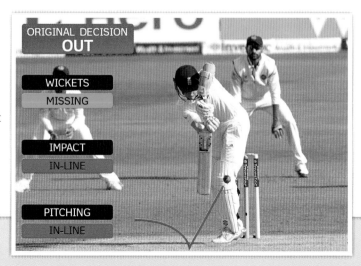

ORIGINAL DECISION
OUT

WICKETS
MISSING

IMPACT
IN-LINE

PITCHING
IN-LINE

Is it reliable?

Manufacturers claim that the average error in tennis is 3.6 mm (about the width of the fluff on the ball) and that the error is lower closer to the lines because that is where the technology is focused on. However, the computer prediction is relied on when a player makes a challenge – so if the computer says the ball is 1 mm out then it is called out even though that is much less than the reported margin of error.

Is it a good thing for sport?

- It is not all good or all bad, so the answer to this is a matter of opinion. The accuracy of the technology is likely to improve with time because computers will be able to process data more quickly and the costs will reduce.

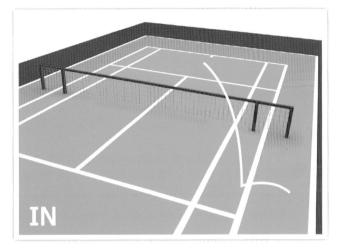

- Things to consider:
  - When is a decision challenged?
  - Are strategic challenges made?
  - What are the consequences of right/wrong decisions?

- The tennis scoring system is such that those 'big points', such as a game point or a match point, might have a huge influence on the outcome of the match!

A force is an influence that can cause a change in the motion of a body, or cause a stationary body to move. Intuitively, we recognise the concept of force as a 'push' or 'pull'. We encounter forces all the time in everyday life, such as when pulling a sledge up a hill or pushing a trolley in the supermarket. The physical quantity of force is important in most mechanical applications.

Objectives
- Identify the forces acting in a given situation.
- Understand the vector nature of force, and find and use components and resultants.
- Use the principle that, when a particle is in equilibrium, the resultant of the forces acting is zero, or, equivalently, that the sum of the components in any direction is zero.

Before you start
You should know how to:

1. Use trigonometry to find angles and side lengths in right-angled triangles.
   - $\sin \theta = \dfrac{\text{opposite}}{\text{hypotenuse}}$
   - $\cos \theta = \dfrac{\text{adjacent}}{\text{hypotenuse}}$
   - $\tan \theta = \dfrac{\text{opposite}}{\text{adjacent}}$

2. Use the **sine rule**, which relates the angles and sides of a triangle, **e.g.**

   $\dfrac{a}{\sin A} = \dfrac{b}{\sin 58} = \dfrac{3.2}{\sin 42}$

   $b = 4.06 \text{ cm}$

Skills check:

1. Raj walks 6 km west from point A to point B in a straight line. He then returns to A from where he walks 8 km north to a point C. From C he returns directly to B. Find the angle between AB and BC.

2. Calculate the length of BC.

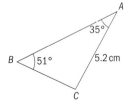

3. Use the cosine rule, which relates the angles and sides of a triangle, **e.g.**

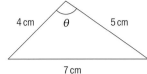

$c^2 = a^2 + b^2 - 2ab \cos C$

$c^2 = 9.5^2 + 4.2^2 - 2 \times 9.5$
$\qquad \times 4.2 \times \cos 37$

$c^2 = 44.1589...$

$\quad c = 6.65 \, \text{cm} \ (3 \, \text{s.f.})$

3. Find angle θ.

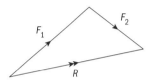

4.1 Resultants

A force has both magnitude and direction, which means it is a vector quantity. The magnitude of a force is measured in newtons (N).

To find the combined effect of a number of forces we can use the triangle rule, placing the start of the second force at the end of the first.

In the diagram, F_1 is combined with F_2 by placing F_2 at the end of F_1. The size and direction of the resultant of the two forces, R, are given by the third side of the triangle.

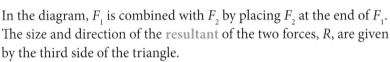

Or we can use the parallelogram rule, placing both forces with the same starting point and completing a parallelogram.

In the diagram the forces F_1 and F_2 are placed together with the same starting point. Their resultant R is the diagonal of the parallelogram.

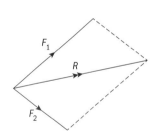

Example 1

An anchor is being pulled using ropes by two sailors with forces of 40 N and 60 N, as shown in the diagram. The angle between the two forces is 30°.

Find the magnitude and direction of the resultant of the two forces.

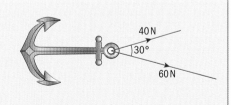

- -

Place the 60 N force at the end of the 40 N force and complete the triangle of forces. The angle between the two forces will be $180° - 30° = 150°$.

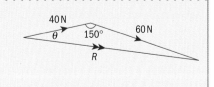

The magnitude of the resultant R is given by the third side of the triangle and its direction is given by θ in the diagram.

▶ Continued on the next page

Using the cosine rule:

$$R^2 = 40^2 + 60^2 - 2 \times 40 \times 60 \times \cos 150°$$

$$R = 96.7312...\,N$$

$$R \approx 96.7\,N$$

Using the sine rule:

$$\frac{96.7}{\sin 150°} = \frac{40}{\sin \theta}$$

$$\theta \approx 11.9°$$

Example 2

A boat is being towed along a canal by cables that are attached to two horses. The stronger horse produces a force of 300 N and the other produces a force of 260 N, as shown in the diagram.

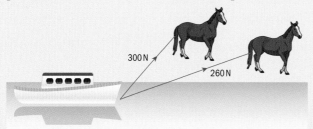

Find the acute angle between the two forces if their resultant has a magnitude of 540 N.

Place the 260 N force at the end of the 300 N force and complete the triangle of forces with the resultant of 540 N. The angle between the forces is θ, as shown in the diagram.

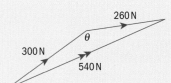

Using the cosine rule:

$$\cos\theta = \frac{260^2 + 300^2 - 540^2}{2 \times 260 \times 300}$$

$$\theta = 149.202...°$$

$$\theta \approx 149°$$

Hence the acute angle between the two forces is $180° - 149.202...° \approx 30.8°$.

Exercise 4.1

1. A small car that has broken down is being pulled by two ropes attached to the front of the car. The forces pulling on the ropes are 10 N and 12 N. Find the magnitude of the resultant force and its direction when the angle between the ropes is

   a) 20° b) 45° c) 105°.

2. Two horses are pulling a cart. The following four diagrams show the forces being applied by the horses at different times. For each diagram, calculate the magnitude of their resultant and the angle it makes with the larger of the two forces.

a)

210 N

30°

300 N

b)

150 N

200 N

c)

45°

500 N

420 N

d)

160 N

190 N

125°

3. A tractor has broken down and is being pushed by two people who exert forces parallel to the direction of motion of the tractor and in the same vertical plane. The forces are 210 N, 15° above the horizontal, and 190 N, 35° below the horizontal, as shown in the diagram.

Find the resultant of the two forces.

210 N

15°

35°

190 N

4. Two tug boats are towing a ship into harbour. One of the boats produces a pulling force of 25 000 N. The other produces a pulling force of 27 000 N. Their resultant has a magnitude of 35 000 N. Find the angle between the two forces and the angle the resultant makes with the larger of the two forces.

5. A young boy is being pulled along on a sledge by both of his parents. In order for the sledge to move along the snow, two forces of 120 N and X N, with an angle of 65° between them, have to be maintained. If the resultant of the two forces has a magnitude of 160 N, find the value of X.

6. A caravan has just been sold at a garage, but the equipment needed to remove it has broken down. Instead, the new owner and the salesperson have decided to push the caravan to the forecourt of the garage so that the owner can connect it to his car and drive it away.

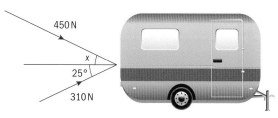

The diagram shows a force of 450 N being applied in the direction of motion of the caravan at an angle x above the horizontal and a second force of 310 N being applied at an angle of 25° below the horizontal; both forces are applied in the same vertical plane. If the magnitude of the resultant of the two forces is 620 N, find the angle x between the 450 N force and the horizontal.

4.2 Components

Previously we have looked at combining two forces into a single force (called the resultant). We will now look at the reverse process, which involves taking a single force and breaking it up into **components**. In this process we **resolve** the force into two components (or resolved parts) in perpendicular directions.

To resolve a force in two perpendicular directions, consider the diagram on the right.

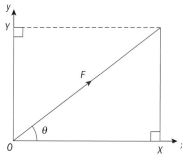

$$\cos \theta = \frac{OX}{F}, \text{ giving } OX = F \cos \theta$$

$$\sin \theta = \frac{OY}{F}, \text{ giving } OY = F \sin \theta$$

> The force in the x-direction, OX, is $F \cos \theta$ and in the y-direction, OY, is $F \sin \theta$.

A force in the x-direction is regarded as the horizontal component and a force in the y-direction is regarded as the vertical component.

Example 3

Using the diagram, find the components of the given force in the direction of

a) the x-axis

b) the y-axis.

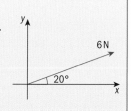

. . . .

a) Along the x-axis, component $OX = 6 \times \cos 20° \approx 5.64$ N

b) Along the y-axis, component $OY = 6 \times \sin 20° \approx 2.05$ N

Exercise 4.2

For each of the following diagrams, find the components of the given force in the direction of

    a) the x-axis   **b)** the y-axis.

1.
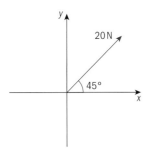

2.
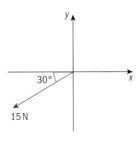

3.
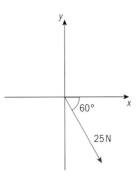

4.
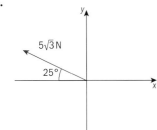

5.
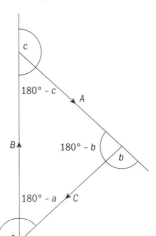

4.3 Forces in equilibrium

A body, and the forces acting upon it, is in **equilibrium** if the body is at rest or is moving with constant velocity. In the diagram, three forces A, B and C are acting on a particle that is in equilibrium. The angles between these forces are a, b and c, as shown on the far right.

Since the three forces are in equilibrium their resultant is zero, and hence the vector diagram, drawn nose-to-tail, is a closed triangle.

Using the sine rule in the triangle:

$$\frac{A}{\sin(180-a)} = \frac{B}{\sin(180-b)} = \frac{C}{\sin(180-c)}$$

Since $\sin(180-a) = \sin a$ we get

$$\frac{A}{\sin a} = \frac{B}{\sin b} = \frac{C}{\sin c}$$

Note: This relationship is known as Lami's theorem. It can give a neat solution to problems involving three forces in equilibrium, as an alternative to resolving forces.

When the resultant of a number of forces is zero, it follows that the sum of the components in any direction is zero. When solving problems we will look at, for example, the sum of the components of forces in the horizontal and vertical directions or at the sum of the components of forces parallel and perpendicular to a slope.

Example 4

A mass of 10 kg is suspended in equilibrium by two light inextensible strings A and B, which make angles of 15° and 35°, respectively, to the horizontal, as shown in the diagram. Calculate the tensions in the strings.

Take $g = 10\,\text{m s}^{-2}$.

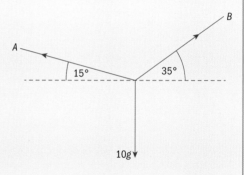

Resolving horizontally and vertically:

$A\cos 15° = B\cos 35°$ (1)

$A\sin 15° + B\sin 35° = 10g$ (2)

Solving (1):

$$A = \frac{B\cos 35°}{\cos 15°} \qquad (3)$$

Substituting (3) into (2):

$$\frac{B\cos 35°}{\cos 15°} \times \sin 15° + B\sin 35° = 10g$$

$B \approx 126\,\text{N}$

Substituting B into (3):

$A \approx 107\,\text{N}$

Alternatively, using Lami's theorem:

From the diagram given, the angles between the forces are $15° + 90° = 105°$, $35° + 90° = 125°$ and $360° - 105° - 125° = 130°$, hence

▶ Continued on the next page

$$\frac{A}{\sin 125°} = \frac{B}{\sin 105°} = \frac{10g}{\sin 130°}$$

$$A = \frac{\sin 125° \times 10g}{\sin 130°} \approx 107\,\text{N}$$

$$B = \frac{\sin 105° \times 10g}{\sin 130°} \approx 126\,\text{N}$$

A similar approach would involve the use of the triangle of forces.

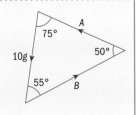

Example 5

Three forces of 15 N, 8 N and X N on a particle keep it in equilibrium, as shown in the diagram.
Find X and θ.

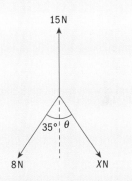

Resolving horizontally and vertically:

$8\sin 35° = X\sin\theta$ (1)

$8\cos 35° + X\cos\theta = 15$ (2)

Rearranging (1):

$$X = \frac{8\sin 35°}{\sin\theta} \qquad (3)$$

Substituting for X in (2):

$$8\cos 35° + \frac{8\sin 35°}{\sin\theta}\cos\theta = 15$$

$$\tan\theta = \frac{8\sin 35°}{15 - 8\cos 35°}$$

$\theta \approx 28.5°$

Substituting for θ in (3):

$X \approx 9.61\,\text{N}$

▶ Continued on the next page

In this example with an unknown force and angle, Lami's theorem does not provide a result easily. Instead the triangle of forces can be used, as shown.

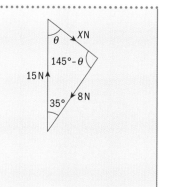

Using the cosine rule:

$X^2 = 15^2 + 8^2 - 2 \times 15 \times 8 \cos 35°$

$X \approx 9.61$ N

$\cos\theta = \dfrac{15^2 + 9.61^2 - 8^2}{2 \times 15 \times 9.61}$

$\theta \approx 28.5°$

In cases where there are more than three forces acting, a triangle of forces is not appropriate. The triangle could be replaced by a polygon of forces. However, in these cases it is usually more efficient to resolve forces.

Example 6

A particle of mass 4 kg is suspended in equilibrium from two light inextensible strings that are at angles of 52° and 46° to the vertical. Calculate the tensions T_1 and T_2 in the two strings.

Take $g = 10 \, \text{m s}^{-2}$.

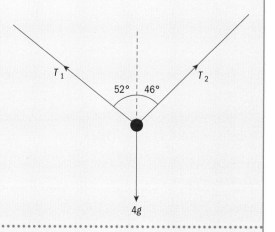

Resolving horizontally:

$T_1 \sin 52° = T_2 \sin 46°$

$\Rightarrow T_2 = \dfrac{T_1 \sin 52°}{\sin 46°}$

Resolving vertically:

$T_1 \cos 52° + T_2 \cos 46° = 4g$

Substituting for T_2:

$T_1 \cos 52° + \dfrac{T_1 \sin 52°}{\sin 46°} \cos 46° = 40$

$T_1 \approx 29.1 \, \text{N}$

$T_2 \approx 31.8 \, \text{N}$

Exercise 4.3

1. Each of the following systems of forces is in equilibrium. For each one, find the magnitude of the missing forces and, where appropriate, the size of angle θ.

a)

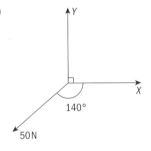

b)

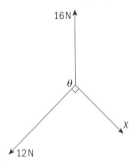

c)

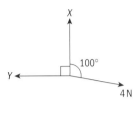

d)

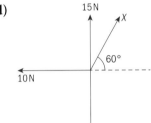

e)

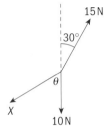

f)

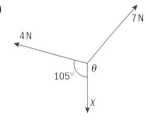

g)

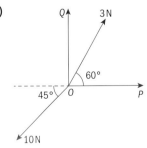

2. The forces acting at O cause the system to be in equilibrium. By resolving, find P and Q.

a)

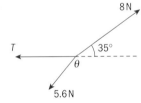

b)

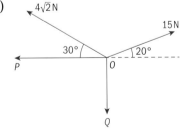

c)

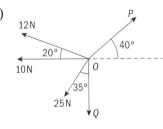

3. Three horses are tethered by light horizontal ropes to a smooth light ring that is 1 m above the ground in the middle of a flat field. Each horse is pulling on the ring, which is in equilibrium. The horses are pulling in the directions N, SE and SW. The first horse is pulling with a force of 80 N. Find the forces that the other horses are pulling with.

4. A particle of weight 15 N is attached to one end of a light inextensible string whose other end is fixed. The particle is pulled aside by a horizontal force F that holds the string at an angle of 30° to the vertical. Find the magnitudes of the tension in the string and the horizontal force.

5. A spring in a horizontal pipe pushes against a light ball with a horizontal force of TN. In order to prevent the ball from being thrown out of the pipe, two people apply forces against the ball bearing, holding it in equilibrium. One person applies a force of 10 N at an angle of 20° above the horizontal and the other a force of FN at an angle of 15° below the horizontal. Calculate the values of T and F.

6.

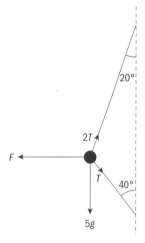

A particle of mass 5 kg is attached to two fixed points on a vertical wall by two light inextensible strings. The particle is held in equilibrium, with the strings taut, by a horizontal force F. The strings are at angles of 20° and 40° to the wall, as shown in the diagram, and the tension in the upper string is twice that in the lower string. Calculate the tensions in the strings and the magnitude of the horizontal force F.

Summary exercise 4

1. For each system of forces shown in each of the following diagrams, find the components of the resultant force in the direction of

   a) the x-axis   b) the y-axis.

   c) Calculate the magnitude of the resultant force.

   i)

   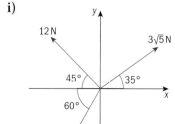

ii)

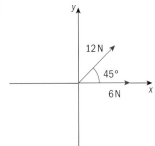

iii)

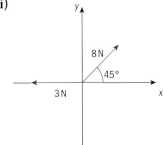

iv)

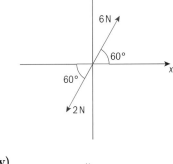

v)

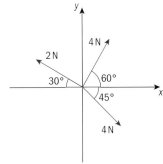

vi)

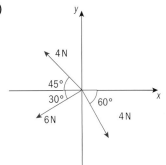

vii)

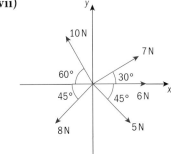

2. For each of the following system of forces, find the magnitude of the resultant.

a)

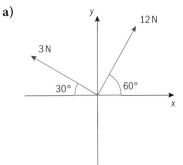

b)

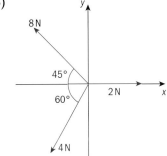

c)

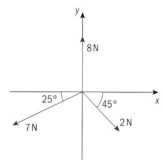

d)

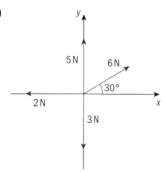

c)

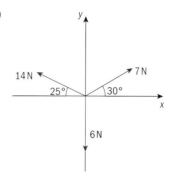

d)

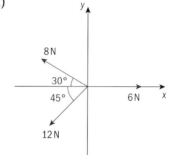

3. For the following combinations of forces, find the resultant and the angle it makes with the positive *x*-axis.

a)

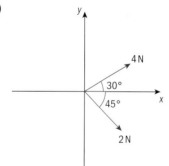

b)

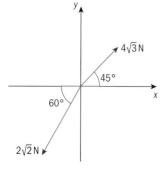

4. Each of the following systems of forces is in equilibrium. Find the magnitude of *X*.

a)

30 N

45°

50 N

X

b)

35 N

25 N   120°

X

c) 10 N

7 N

X

d)

X

16 N

50°

25 N

e)

x

12 N

60°

15√3 N

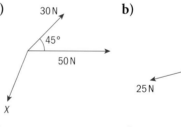

f)

x

40 N

60°

50 N

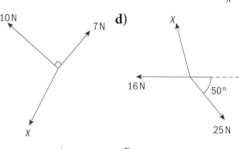

5. The forces acting at O cause the system to be in equilibrium. By resolving in two directions, find A and B.

a)   **b)**

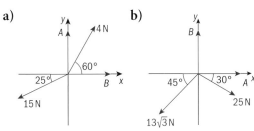

c)   **d)**

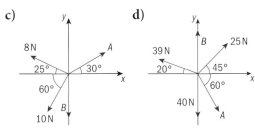

6. The angle between two forces of 350 N and 250 N is 35°. Find their resultant.

7. The angle between a force of 47 N and 56 N is 90°. Find their resultant.

8. The angle between a force of 200 N and X N is 20°. Given that their resultant has magnitude of 367.4 N, find the value of X.

9. Find the magnitude of X, given that the resultant between the forces of 8 N and X N is $\sqrt{97}$ N and the angle between the two forces is 60°.

10. Find the angle between a force of 10 N and 9 N, given that their resultant has magnitude 17.86 N.

11. The angle between a force of 5 N and X N is 90°. Given that their resultant has a magnitude of $\sqrt{55}$ N, find the value of X.

12. The following diagram shows a particle in equilibrium under the forces shown.

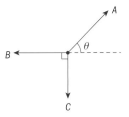

Show that $C = B \tan \theta$.

13. The following diagram shows a particle in equilibrium under the forces shown.

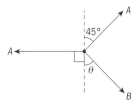

Show that $\tan \theta = \sqrt{2} - 1$.

EXAM-STYLE QUESTION

14.

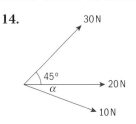

Coplanar forces of magnitude 30 N, 20 N and 10 N act at a point in the directions shown in the diagram. Given that $\sin \alpha = \dfrac{5}{13}$, find the magnitude and the direction of the resultant of the three forces.

15.

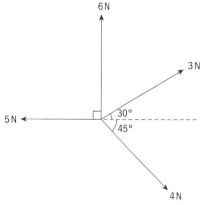

Four coplanar forces act at a point. The magnitudes of the forces are 5 N, 6 N, 3 N and 4 N, and the directions in which the forces act are shown in the diagram. Find the magnitude and direction of the resultant of the four forces.

16.

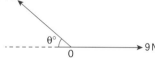

Forces of magnitudes 7 N and 9 N act at a point O in the directions shown in the diagram. The resultant of these forces has magnitude 11 N. Find the value of θ and the component of the resultant in the direction of the force of magnitude 9 N.

17.

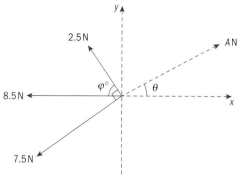

Coplanar forces of magnitudes 8.5 N, 2.5 N, A N and 7.5 N act at a point in the directions shown in the diagram. The system is in equilibrium. Given that $\tan \varphi = \dfrac{4}{3}$, find the values of A and θ.

Chapter summary

- The resultant of two forces F_1 and F_2 is found using the triangle (or parallelogram) rule.

- The two perpendicular components of a force F when it is resolved are $F\cos\theta$ and $F\sin\theta$.

- When a particle is in equilibrium, the sum of the components of the forces acting in any direction is zero.

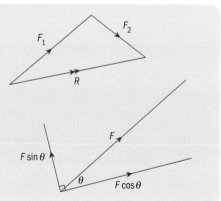

Newton's laws

Soviet cosmonaut Yuri Gagarin became the first human to orbit the Earth. He achieved this in the Vostok spacecraft, which was launched on April 12, 1961. The spaceflight consisted of one orbit and took 108 minutes from launch to landing. At the end of the flight, Gagarin parachuted to the ground separately from his spacecraft after ejecting at an altitude of 7 km. Newton's laws explain how a spacecraft will accelerate back to Earth under the influence of gravity after being launched by a powerful force. We can also use Newton's laws to show the exact speed a spacecraft will need to achieve to go into orbit.

Objectives

- Use Newton's third law.
- Apply Newton's laws of motion to the linear motion of a particle of constant mass moving under the action of constant forces, which may include friction, tension in an inextensible string or thrust in a connecting rod.
- Use the relationship between mass and weight.
- Solve simple problems that may be modelled as the motion of a particle moving vertically or on a slope with constant acceleration.
- Solve simple problems that may be modelled as the motion of connected particles.

Before you start

You should know how to:

1. Use the constant acceleration formulae.

$$v = u + at \qquad v^2 = u^2 + 2as$$
$$s = ut + \frac{1}{2}at^2 \qquad s = \frac{1}{2}(u + v)t$$

   e.g. Find s when $v = 15\,\mathrm{m\,s^{-1}}$, $u = 3\,\mathrm{m\,s^{-1}}$ and $a = 3\,\mathrm{m\,s^{-2}}$.
   $$15^2 = 3^2 - 2 \times 3 \times s; \qquad s = 36\,\mathrm{m}$$

2. Resolve forces in perpendicular directions.
   e.g. Find the horizontal and vertical components of a force of 15 N at an angle of 30° to the horizontal.
   Horizontal: $15\cos 30° = 13.0\,\mathrm{N}$;
   Vertical: $15\sin 30° = 7.5\,\mathrm{N}$.

Skills check:

1. **a)** Find s when $t = 2$, $u = 7$ and $a = 5$.
    b) Find u when $v = 36$, $t = 3$ and $a = 8$.
    c) Find s when $u = 5$, $v = 10$ and $a = 15$.

2. Find the horizontal and vertical components of a force of 12 N at 30° above the horizontal.

5.1 Newton's laws

In ancient Greece the universe was understood in terms of the theories of Aristotle and Ptolemy. In their understanding the Earth was at the centre of the universe. This view was held in the Western world until it was challenged by **Nicolaus Copernicus (1473–1543)**, who first understood how the Earth revolved around the Sun, **Johannes Kepler (1571–1630)** who studied planetary motion, and **René Descartes (1596–1650)** who applied mathematical principles to mechanical theory.

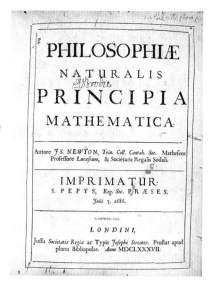

Finally, classical mechanics, the study of the motion of bodies, was founded by **Sir Isaac Newton's** publication of *Philosophiæ Naturalis Principia Mathematica* (1687). In this book, Newton first stated his three laws of motion. Newton's laws have been used now for over three centuries. These laws have been restated and added to, and new theories such as those of quantum physics have emerged. Newton's laws, however, are still the cornerstones of mechanics.

> **Newton's first law** states that every body remains in a state of rest or of uniform motion in a straight line unless an external force acts on it.

This means that if a car is parked in the street it will not move unless it is acted on by the thrust of the engine, or it is pushed or blown along by a hurricane, for example. So why does the driver need to keep their foot down on the accelerator pedal in order to maintain uniform motion? It is because the force is the resultant of all the forces acting on the car. There is the resistance of the road, the force due to gravity if the car is travelling up a hill, and so on.

> **Newton's second law** states that the resultant of the forces acting on a body is equal to the mass of the body multiplied by its acceleration in the direction of that force.

This law can be stated as $F = ma$. More properly, both F and a should be vectors (i.e. they have both magnitude and direction).

One **newton** is defined as the force that is needed to give a mass of 1 kg an acceleration of $1\,\mathrm{m\,s^{-2}}$.

The **weight** of an object is the force that gravity exerts on it. A free-falling object, that is, an object falling solely under the influence of gravity, has an acceleration of approximately $10\,\mathrm{m\,s^{-2}}$ downwards towards the Earth.

This value, the **acceleration due to gravity**, is known as *g*. There are slight variations of this value, due mainly to altitude. The value would also be different, for example, on the Moon.

The weight of an object of mass *m* is then *mg* according to Newton's second law. The units of weight are the same as the units of a force – newtons. Hence a body of mass 20 kg will have a weight of 200 N.

> **Newton's third law** states that to every action there is an equal and opposite reaction.

A car parked on a horizontal street produces a force, equal to its weight, acting downwards on the surface of the street. The car is prevented from disappearing through the surface by an equal and opposite reaction force, *R*, from the street on the car. *R* is called the **normal reaction**. In this case, *R* = *mg*.

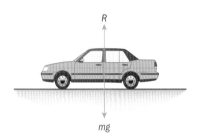

Note: In mechanics we talk about **bodies**, for example, a cricket ball, a car or a spacecraft. Strictly, Newton's three laws apply to **particles**; however, we use them for most cases involving bodies because they work well enough in most situations and are easy to calculate.

Did you know?

According to legend, Newton discovered the universal law of gravitation when he was hit on the head by an apple while sitting under a tree. Like all legends it may not be entirely true, but Newton did come up with some important ideas about gravity. The most important for us is that the **acceleration due to gravity** of all objects near the Earth's surface is a constant, *g*, which is approximately $9.81 \, \text{m s}^{-2}$, and we often round this value up to $10 \, \text{m s}^{-2}$ in calculations.

The Italian scientist and philosopher **Galileo Galilei (1564–1642)** had shown by dropping two balls of different masses from the Leaning Tower of Pisa that the times they took to reach the ground (and thus their acceleration) were the same. Therefore the acceleration is independent of the mass of the body falling. However, the value of *g* would be different on the Moon or on a spacecraft orbiting the Earth.

Example 1

A passenger of mass 60 kg is in a lift of mass 500 kg. The lift is operated by a cable, as shown in the diagram. **Calculate**

a) the force R exerted by the floor of the lift on the passenger

b) the tension T in the cable when the lift is accelerating at 2 m s^{-2} upwards. Take the value of g as 10 m s^{-2}.

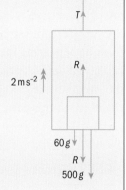

Applying Newton's third law, if the force exerted by the floor of the lift on the passenger is R then there is an equal and opposite force R exerted by the passenger on the floor.

a) Applying Newton's second law for the passenger:

$$R - 60g = 60 \times 2$$

$$R = 720 \text{ N}$$

b) Applying Newton's second law for the lift:

$$T - R - 500g = 500 \times 2$$

$$T = 6720 \text{ N}$$

In Example 1 we used a very important result to do with the weight of a particle.

The mass m of a particle is measured in kg. The weight of that body is a force, mg, and is measured in newtons. As stated previously, 1 N is the force that would give a mass of 1 kg an acceleration of 1 m s^{-2}. The weight of a particle could change if it moved somewhere where the acceleration due to gravity was different. Its mass, however, does not change. An astronaut in space could become weightless, but he or she would still have the same mass as they do on Earth.

In Example 2 and Exercise 5.1 we look at situations where forces act either horizontally or vertically.

Example 2

A particle of mass 3 kg rests on a smooth plane. It is pulled by a horizontal force of 4 N.

Taking the value of g as 10 m s^{-2}, calculate

a) the horizontal acceleration of the particle, a

b) the normal reaction, R.

▶ Continued on the next page

a) Applying Newton's second law horizontally:
$$4 = 3a$$
$$a \approx 1.33\,\mathrm{m\,s^{-2}}$$

b) $W = 3g$
$$= 30\,\mathrm{N}$$
Applying Newton's second law vertically:
$$R - W = 0$$
$$R = 30\,\mathrm{N}$$

Exercise 5.1

1. An ice cube rests on a smooth horizontal table in the carriage of a stationary train. **Explain** what will happen to the ice cube when the train

   a) accelerates out of the station

   b) is travelling at constant velocity

   c) decelerates on approach to the next station.

2. A sledge stands on smooth horizontal icy ground. The sledge has a mass of 35 kg. If a force of 105 N acts on the sledge, find its acceleration.

3. A man pushes a box on horizontal ground with a force of 240 N. There is a frictional force of 60 N opposing the motion. If the acceleration of the box is 12 m s^{-2} while it is being projected, calculate the mass of the box in kg.

4. In the game of curling, a heavy granite stone of mass 20 kg is projected across an ice rink. Ignoring friction, if the acceleration of the stone is 2.4 m s^{-2}, calculate the magnitude of the force projecting it.

5. A wooden block of mass 5 kg is at rest on a smooth horizontal table, 1.6 m from the edge of the table. The block is pulled directly towards the edge by a horizontal string. The tension in the string is 1 N. Calculate the time taken to reach the edge of the table.

6. A small seaplane of mass 8000 kg is travelling with a horizontal speed u m s^{-1} when it lands on the sea. The plane is brought to rest by water resistance of 960 N in 600 m. Calculate the value of u.

7. A toy car of mass 0.35 kg is moving at a velocity of 2 m s^{-1} and comes to rest after it has travelled 3.5 m in a straight line on a horizontal floor. Calculate the resistance force that slows the car down.

8. A porter at a railway station is dragging a suitcase of mass 82.5 kg along the platform with an acceleration of 0.175 m s⁻². The horizontal force that he exerts is 170 N. Find the frictional force between the floor and the trunk.

9. A particle of mass 2.5 kg is pulled in a straight line along a horizontal surface by a string parallel to the surface with an acceleration of 2.8 m s⁻². Given that there is a frictional force of 4 N that opposes the motion of the particle, find the tension in the string. When the particle is travelling at a speed of 3 m s⁻¹, the string breaks. Calculate how much further the particle will travel before coming to rest.

10. A goods lift has a mass of 750 kg and can hold a maximum load of 1200 kg. The lift is raised and lowered by a cable. Using $g = 10 \, \text{m s}^{-2}$, calculate

   a) the tension in the cable when it is being raised with a full load and an acceleration of 0.5 m s⁻²

   b) the tension in the cable when the empty lift is being lowered with an acceleration of 0.7 m s⁻²

   c) the mass of the load if there is a tension of 15 200 N when the partially loaded lift is being raised at a constant speed.

5.2 Resolving components of the weight when on a slope

In Section 4.2 we resolved a single force into two perpendicular components. We are now going to take this idea and apply it to the weight of a body that is resting on a slope.

A body of mass m rests on a plane inclined at an angle θ to the horizontal. The weight of the body is mg acting downwards, where g is the acceleration due to gravity.

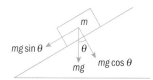

We are going to resolve the weight of the body into two components parallel to and perpendicular to the plane.

Look carefully at the two equal angles in the triangle below the force diagram. The angle of inclination of the plane is equal to the angle between the downward vertical and the perpendicular to the plane.

The two components of the weight are:

$mg \cos \theta$ perpendicular to the plane, and

$mg \sin \theta$ parallel to the plane.

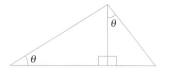

Example 3

A body of mass 10 kg rests on a plane that is inclined at an angle of 30° to the horizontal.

Find the components of the weight of the body

a) parallel to the plane

b) perpendicular to the plane.

(Take g as $10\,\mathrm{m\,s^{-2}}$.)

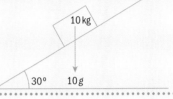

The weight of the body is $10 \times 10 = 100\,\mathrm{N}$

a) Component parallel to the plane:

$100\sin 30° = 50\,\mathrm{N}$

b) Component perpendicular to the plane:

$100\cos 30° = 86.6\,\mathrm{N}$ (3 s.f.)

In the following exercise, take g as $10\,\mathrm{m\,s^{-2}}$.

Exercise 5.2

1. A truck carrying fruit for the local market breaks down on a hill. Given that the truck and fruit have a combined mass of 1500 kg, calculate the components of the weight parallel and perpendicular to the plane of the hill if the hill is inclined at an angle of 5° to the horizontal.

2. A bookseller is delivering some heavy books. While out on her journey she stops to talk to a customer. As she does this the box containing the books, which has a mass of 200 kg, is at rest on a hill. Given that the force acting on the box parallel to the hill is 407.51 N, find the angle of incline.

3. A car with three passengers on board is being driven up a hill when it suddenly breaks down. The hill is inclined at 20°. If the total mass of the car, passengers and driver is 2200 kg, calculate the components of the weight parallel and perpendicular to the hill.

   One by one, each passenger gets out of the car and does not come back (the driver remains in the car). The mass of each passenger in the order they leave the car is 220 kg, 190 kg and 150 kg, respectively.

   a) Find the components of weight both down the hill and perpendicular to the hill after *each* person has left the car.

   b) Find the difference between the initial force perpendicular to the hill and the final force perpendicular to the hill.

4. A skier falls while skiing down a slope that is inclined at 60° to the horizontal, and is left lying on the ground. The component of her weight parallel to and acting down the slope is 780 N. What is the mass of the skier?

5.3 Multiple forces

In Section 5.1 we looked at the motion of a particle or a body when acted on by forces in one direction only. When the forces act in different directions it is necessary to resolve the forces to be able to calculate their effect. In some cases we resolve them horizontally and vertically, and in other cases we might look at forces acting up and perpendicular to a plane.

Example 4

A particle of mass 25 kg rests on a smooth slope that is at 31° to the horizontal. It is pulled by a force of 300 N up the plane.

Taking the value of g as $10\,\mathrm{m\,s^{-2}}$, calculate

a) the acceleration of the particle up the plane, a

b) the normal reaction, R.

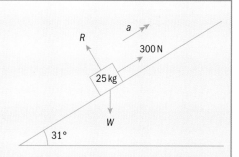

a) $W = mg$

$\qquad = 25 \times 10$

$\qquad = 250\,\mathrm{N}$

Resolving forces up the plane, using Newton's second law:

$300 - 250 \times \sin 31° = 25a$

$171.2 = 25a$

$a \approx 6.85\,\mathrm{m\,s^{-2}}$

b) Resolving forces perpendicular to the plane, using Newton's third law:

$R = 250 \cos 31°$

$\qquad \approx 214\,\mathrm{N}$

Exercise 5.3

1. The diagram shows the forces, all in newtons, that act on an object that is at rest. Find the values of the forces marked P and Q.

a)

b)

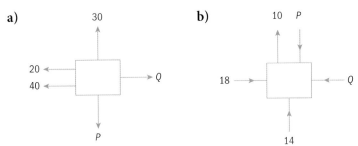

2. A box is being pulled up a smooth slope with an acceleration a by a light inextensible string. Draw a diagram showing all the forces that are acting on the box.

3. A block of mass 5 kg rests on a rough horizontal plane. It is attached to a string that is inclined at an angle of $30°$ to the horizontal, and the tension in the string is 27 N. Find the frictional force acting on the block.

4. A small block of mass 3 kg is being pulled up the line of greatest slope of a rough plane by a string that is parallel to the slope. The slope is inclined at $30°$ to the horizontal. A frictional force of 2.5 N opposes the motion of the block. If the block accelerates at $0.5\,\mathrm{m\,s^{-2}}$, calculate, in terms of g, the tension in the string.

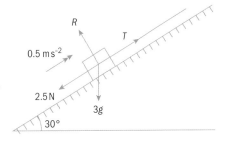

5. A boat is being pulled along a canal by two horizontal cables attached to two horses. The mass of the boat is 800 kg. One horse pulls with a force of 35 N, and the cable is at an angle of $10°$ to the banks of the canal. The other horse pulls with a force of 40 N. Ignoring any resistance to motion, find the angle that the second horse should pull at in order that the boat moves forwards and does not get dragged sideways. Ignoring any frictional resistance, find the acceleration of the boat.

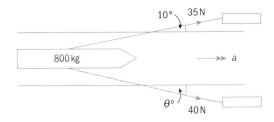

6. A body of mass 5 kg is released from rest so that it slides down the line of greatest slope of a smooth plane inclined at an angle of 25° to the horizontal. It is connected to a light inextensible a rope that is inclined to the plane at an angle of 10°. The tension in the rope is 8 N. Taking g as $10\,\text{m}\,\text{s}^{-2}$, calculate how far it will travel in 6 s.

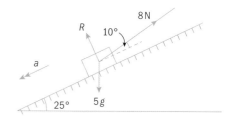

7. A paraglider of mass 85 kg is pulled by a rope attached to a speedboat. With the rope making an angle of 20° to the horizontal the paraglider moves in a straight line parallel to the water surface with an acceleration of $1.5\,\text{m}\,\text{s}^{-2}$. The tension in the rope is 240 N. Taking g as $10\,\text{m}\,\text{s}^{-2}$, calculate the magnitude of the vertical lift force acting on the glider and the magnitude of the air resistance.

5.4 Connected particles

In this section we look at particles connected by a light inextensible string that passes over a smooth pulley and cars towing a trailer by means of either a light rope or a light rigid tow-bar.

- A **light inextensible string** is a string whose length remains the same whether motion is taking place or not.
- A **pulley** is a wheel over which a string passes. A **smooth pulley** has no friction in its bearings.
- A car and trailer can be assumed to behave like two particles connected by a **light rigid tow-bar**.

Note: Friction will be discussed in Chapter 6.

In real-life, strings are not always light and inextensible, not all pulleys are smooth, and cars and trailers do not behave in the same way as particles. But we make these assumptions when modelling, to make calculations more manageable. In these examples the forces acting on the particles are their weight and the tension in the string or the thrust in a connecting rod or tow-bar. When a light inextensible string passes over a smooth light pulley or over a smooth peg the tension in the string either side of the pulley will be the same, i.e. the tension will be constant along its length. We also find that, because the particles are connected, their acceleration will have the same magnitude, but in opposite directions.

Example 5

Two particles of mass 5 kg and 7 kg are connected by a light, inextensible string, which hangs over a smooth, light pulley.

Taking the value of g as $10 \, \text{m s}^{-2}$, calculate

a) the weights of the two particles, W_1 and W_2
b) the acceleration of the system, a
c) the normal reaction at the point where the pulley is suspended, R.

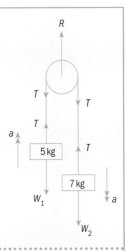

a) $W_1 = 5g$
  $= 5 \times 10 = 50 \, \text{N}$
  $W_2 = 7g$
  $= 7 \times 10 = 70 \, \text{N}$

b) Resolving forces vertically for each of the particles:

  $T - 50 = 5a$
  $70 - T = 7a$
  $20 = 12a$
  $a \approx 1.67 \, \text{m s}^{-2}$

c) $R = 2T$
  $= 2 \times (50 + 5 \times 1.67)$
  $\approx 117 \, \text{N}$

Example 6

A car of mass 1000 kg is pulling a trailer of mass 800 kg down a line of greatest slope of a hill. The hill is inclined at an angle of θ to the horizontal, where $\sin \theta = 0.05$. The car and the trailer are connected by a light, rigid tow-bar, which is parallel to the road. The driving force of the car's engine is 2000 N, the resistance to the car is 400 N, and the resistance to the trailer is 100 N. Find

a) the acceleration of the system
b) the tension in the tow-bar.

(Take g as $10 \, \text{m s}^{-2}$.)

▶ Continued on the next page

a) Resolving forces and applying Newton's second law parallel to the plane of the hill for the system:

$$2000 + 1000g \times 0.05 - 400$$
$$+ 800g \times 0.05 - 100 = 1800a$$
$$2400 = 1800a$$
$$a \approx 1.33 \text{ m s}^{-2}$$

b) Resolving forces and applying Newton's second law parallel to the plane of the hill for the car:

$$2000 + 1000g \times 0.05 - 400 - T = 1000 \times 1.33$$
$$T \approx 767 \text{ N}$$

or

Resolving forces and applying Newton's second law parallel to the plane of the hill for the trailer:

$$T + 800g \times 0.05 - 100 = 800 \times 1.33$$
$$T \approx 767 \text{ N}$$

Exercise 5.4

1. Two particles of mass 5 kg and 3 kg are being pulled along a horizontal surface. They are connected by a light inextensible string. The resistances to the motion of the particles are 1 N and 2 N, respectively. The 5 kg particle is being pulled by a 7 N force. Find the acceleration of the two particles and the tension in the string.

2. A model train of mass 4 kg is pushing a carriage of mass 1 kg along a horizontal track. They are connected by a light rigid coupling. The resistances to the motion of the train and carriage are 2 N and 3 N, respectively. The train pushes the carriage with a force of 15 N.
   a) Find the acceleration and the force in the coupling.
   b) When the velocity is 0.1 m s^{-1}, the pushing force reduces to 0. Find the time in seconds that elapses before the train and carriage come to rest.

3. Two particles of mass 3 kg and 2 kg are connected by a light inextensible string that passes over a smooth pulley. Find the acceleration of the particles, the tension in the string and the magnitude of the resultant force exerted by the string on the pulley. (Take g as 10 m s^{-2}.)

4. Two particles of mass 2 kg and 8 kg are connected by a light inextensible string that passes over a smooth pulley.
   a) Taking g as 10 m s^{-2}, find the acceleration of the particles and the tension in the string.

   The particles are released from rest with the portions of string that are not in contact with the pulley taut and vertical.

   b) Find the time for their velocity to reach 18 m s^{-1}.

5. Two particles of mass 5 kg and 10 kg are connected by a light
   inextensible string that passes over a smooth pulley.
   a) Taking g as $10 \, \text{m s}^{-2}$, find the acceleration of the particles.

   The particles are released from rest, with the portions of string that are
   not in contact with the pulley taut and vertical, and travel a distance of 15 m.
   b) Find their final velocity.

6. Some repairs are being carried out on a tall building.
   A pulley is attached to the top of the scaffolding and a
   rope runs over the pulley with buckets of mass 2 kg
   attached to each end. One bucket, at the top of the
   building, is filled with rubble of mass 8 kg and released.
   What will be its acceleration? Give your answer
   in terms of g.

7. A small block of mass 4 kg rests on a table and is connected
   by a light inextensible string that passes over a smooth
   pulley fixed to the edge of the table, to another small block
   of mass 2 kg that is hanging freely. If the table is rough
   and exerts a frictional force of $1.5 \, g \, \text{N}$ on the block, find,
   in terms of g, the acceleration of the blocks and the tension
   in the string.

8. A block of mass 15 kg rests on a plane that is inclined at 30°
   to the horizontal. It is connected by a light inextensible string
   that passes over a smooth pulley that is attached to the top of
   the plane to another block of mass 10 kg that is hanging freely.
   If the frictional force exerted by the plane on the block is 2.4 N,
   find the resulting acceleration of the blocks. (Take g as $10 \, \text{m s}^{-2}$.)

9. A shunting engine is pushing a railway carriage on a track up the line of
   greatest slope of a hill that is inclined at an angle of θ to the horizontal,
   where $\sin \theta = 0.02$. The engine and the carriage are connected by a light
   rigid coupling that is parallel to the track. The engine has a mass of
   12 000 kg, and it creates a driving force of 15 000 N. There is a resistance
   of 2000 N to the motion of the engine. The carriage has a mass of 8000 kg,
   and there is a resistance of 1500 N to its motion. Taking g as $10 \, \text{m s}^{-2}$, find
   a) the acceleration of the engine and carriage up the hill
   b) the thrust in the coupling.

10. A funicular railway runs up a steep slope and has two carriages connected by a cable that runs over a pulley at the top of the slope. The weight of one carriage running down the track helps to pull up the second carriage. The mass of each carriage is 10 000 kg, and the track is inclined at an angle of 40° to the horizontal. The resistance to motion felt by each carriage is 100 N. Ignoring the weight of the cable and assuming that the pulley is smooth, calculate the force (labelled F in the diagram) required to pull a carriage up the slope with an acceleration of 2.0 m s^{-2}.

Did you know?
A funicular railway is a type of railway where a cable is used to pull two trams up or down a slope. As one tram ascends, the other descends, and they counterbalance each other.

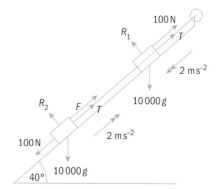

Summary exercise 5

Hint: Use $g = 10$ m s^{-2} where a numerical value is required.

1.

A heavy load is being hauled up on a building site by a rope attached to a pulley. The rope is being pulled at an angle of 40° to the vertical. If the acceleration of the load is 0.25 m s^{-2}, calculate the force with which the rope is being pulled, and the magnitude and direction of the reaction at the point where the pulley is fixed.

2. A lift of mass 750 kg is suspended by a cable. A passenger of mass 65 kg stands in the lift.

a) When the lift is accelerating upwards at 0.4 m s^{-2}, find

   i) the force exerted by the passenger on the floor of the lift

   ii) the tension in the cable.

b) When the lift is accelerating downwards at 0.6 m s^{-2}, find

   i) the force exerted by the passenger on the floor of the lift

   ii) the tension in the cable.

3. A small block of mass 2 kg rests on a horizontal table. It is connected by a light inextensible string that passes over a smooth pulley to another block of mass 3 kg that is hanging freely. If the surface of the table exerts a frictional force of 15 N, calculate the acceleration of the system and the tension in the string.

4. A car of mass 1200 kg moves in a straight line along horizontal ground. The resistance to motion of the car is constant and has a magnitude of 960 N.

   a) Calculate the acceleration of the car when the car's engine is providing a driving force of 1440 N.

   When the car passes through a particular point it is moving with a constant speed of $18\,\mathrm{m\,s^{-1}}$. At that instant the engine fails. The car continues to freewheel in a straight line until it comes to rest.

   b) Find the distance it takes to come to rest.

EXAM-STYLE QUESTIONS

5. A tractor of mass 1500 kg is pulling a trailer of mass 1000 kg up a line of greatest slope of a hill that is inclined at an angle of θ to the horizontal, where $\sin\theta = 0.15$. A light, rigid tow-bar, which is parallel to the road surface, connects the tractor and the trailer. The tractor engine's driving force is 5500 N and the resistances against the tractor and the trailer are 400 N and 200 N, respectively.

   a) Calculate the acceleration of the system and the tension in the tow-bar.

   When the tractor and trailer are travelling at a speed of $25\,\mathrm{m\,s^{-1}}$ the driving force becomes zero.

   b) Find the time, in seconds, before the system comes to rest, and the force in the tow-bar during this time. Explain the sign of the force you have found.

6. A cyclist produces a constant driving force of magnitude $F\,\mathrm{N}$ while moving up a straight hill inclined at an angle θ to the horizontal, where $\sin\theta = \dfrac{28}{175}$. A constant force of 30 N resists the motion of the cyclist. The combined weight of the cyclist and her bicycle is 700 N. The cyclist is decelerating at a rate of $0.15\,\mathrm{m\,s^{-2}}$.

   a) Calculate the value of F.

   At the bottom of the hill the cyclist's speed is $6\,\mathrm{m\,s^{-1}}$.

   b) Find how far up the hill the cyclist travels before she comes to rest.

Chapter summary

Newton's first law

Every body remains in a state of rest or of uniform motion in a straight line unless an external force acts on it.

Newton's second law

The resultant of the forces acting on a body is equal to the mass of the body multiplied by its acceleration in the direction of that force.

Newton's third law

To every action there is an equal and opposite reaction.

- The mass m of a particle is measured in kg. The weight of that body is a force, mg, and is measured in newtons.
- $1\,N$ is the force required to give a mass of $1\,kg$ an acceleration of $1\,m\,s^{-2}$.

Resolving components of the weight when on a slope

- On a slope and perpendicular to the slope, $F = m\,g\cos\theta$.
- On a slope and parallel to the slope, $F = mg\sin\theta$.

Connected particles

When particles are connected by a light inextensible string passing over a smooth pulley, or a car is towing a trailer by means of either a light rope or a light rigid tow-bar:

- the tension along the rope (or the thrust along the tow-bar) will be the same along its whole length
- the acceleration of the particles (or of the car and trailer) will have the same magnitude (but not necessarily the same direction).

6 Friction

Friction is a force that opposes the motion between two surfaces in contact, and is encountered when an object slides on a surface. A smooth surface, for example a pane of glass, offers so little frictional resistance to the motion of the object sliding across it that the friction can sometimes be ignored. But as most real objects on real surfaces experience friction it is an extremely important consideration in most applications of mechanics. Any surface that gives rise to friction is called a 'rough' surface in mechanics.

Objectives

- Understand that a contact force between two surfaces can be represented by two components, the normal component and the frictional component.
- Use the model of a 'smooth' contact, and understand the limitations of this model.
- Understand the concepts of limiting friction and limiting equilibrium; recall the definition of coefficient of friction, and use the relationship $F = \mu R$ or $F \le \mu R$, as appropriate.

Before you start

You should know how to:

1. Use trigonometric ratios to find missing angles.

$$\sin\theta = \frac{\text{opposite}}{\text{hypotenuse}}; \cos\theta = \frac{\text{adjacent}}{\text{hypotenuse}}$$

$$\tan\theta = \frac{\text{opposite}}{\text{adjacent}}$$

e.g.

$$\cos\theta = \frac{\text{adj}}{\text{hyp}}$$

(hyp) 5 cm   (opp)

θ

3 cm (adj)

$$\cos\theta = \frac{3}{5} \Rightarrow \theta = \cos^{-1}\left(\frac{3}{5}\right) = 53.1° \text{ (3s.f.)}$$

Use trigonometric ratios to find missing sides.

$$\sin 35° = \frac{a}{29}$$

$$a = 29 \sin 35°$$

$$= 16.63 \text{ cm}$$

(hyp) 29 cm   (opp) a

35°

Skills check:

1. Find the missing angles in each of the following triangles.

   a) In triangle ABC, $AC = 34$ cm and $AB = 30$ cm.
      $\angle ABC$ is a right angle.
      Find $\cos CAB$ and $\angle CAB$.

   b) In triangle PQR, $PQ = 18$ cm and $RQ = 30$ cm.
      $\angle RPQ$ is a right angle.
      Find $\cos PQR$ and $\angle PQR$.

   c) In the triangle XYZ, which has a right angle at Y, $XY = 15$ cm and $YZ = 20$ cm. Find the length of the longest side. Find $\angle ZXY$.

2. Rearrange the following, making *a* the subject.

e.g. $v^2 = u^2 + 2as$

$$a = \frac{v^2 - u^2}{2s}$$

3. Substituting into formulae.

e.g. Substitute the following values into the equation to find *v*.

$v = u + at$; when $a = 10$, $t = 3$ and $u = 5$

$v = 5 + 10(3)$

$= 35$

2. With the following equations, make the letter in brackets the subject.

a) $v = u + at$ (*a*)

b) $s = ut + \frac{1}{2}at^2$ (*a*)

c) $p^2 = \sqrt{\dfrac{g^3}{t}}$ (*t*)

3. For the following, substitute values into the formulae and solve.

a) $v^2 = u^2 + 2as$; $u = 3$, $a = 5$, $s = 3$

b) $s = ut + \frac{1}{2}at^2$; $u = 0.5$, $t = 3$, $a = 10$

c) $p^2 = \sqrt{\dfrac{g^3}{t}}$; $g = \frac{2}{5}$, $t = \frac{3}{7}$

Frictional forces

Imagine a horizontal force *X* being applied to a heavy object standing on a rough horizontal floor. Friction will oppose the force *X*. As *X* increases, the frictional force also increases, so that they have the same magnitude but in opposite directions, until the frictional force reaches its maximum value, which is denoted by F_{max}.

Note: F_{max} is called the limiting friction.

An object will move when the force being applied is greater than the maximum frictional force.

If $X < F_{max}$ then no motion will take place.

If $X > F_{max}$ then motion will take place.

If $X = F_{max}$ then the object is about to slip.

When the object is about to slip we say it is in the state of limiting equilibrium and

$$F_{max} = \mu R$$

where *R* is the normal reaction and μ is the coefficient of friction (which usually lies between 0 and 1). For surfaces modelled as perfectly smooth there is no friction, and the coefficient of friction is 0. Some surfaces, such as rubber on steel, can be very 'sticky' and have a coefficient of friction much greater than 1.

Note: The Greek letter μ is pronounced 'myew' or 'moo'.

6.1 Rough horizontal surfaces

Example 1

Using the diagram, calculate the maximum frictional force that can act where a child's sledge rests on a rough horizontal surface where the coefficient between the surfaces is

a) 0.1   b) 0.5   c) 0.8

Take *g* as $10\,\mathrm{m\,s^{-2}}$.

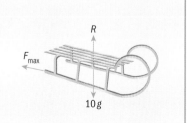

▶ Continued on the next page

As the sledge is at rest, there is no motion perpendicular to the ground.

Resolving vertically:

$R = 10g$

$= 10 \times 10 = 100\,\text{N}$

a) $F_{max} = \mu R$ (maximum frictional force)

$= 0.1 \times 100$

$= 10\,\text{N}$

b) $F_{max} = \mu R$

$= 0.5 \times 100$

$= 50\,\text{N}$

c) $F_{max} = \mu R$

$= 0.8 \times 100$

$= 80\,\text{N}$

In Example 1 we looked at an object at rest. In Example 2 we will explore what happens when parallel forces are applied to an object on a rough horizontal surface.

Example 2

A brick of mass 2 kg is at rest on a rough horizontal surface. The coefficient of friction between the brick and the surface is 0.9.

Calculate the frictional force acting on the brick when a horizontal force X is applied to the brick and its magnitude is

a) 10 N   b) 15 N   c) 35 N.

Calculate the magnitude of any acceleration that takes place due to motion.

Take g as $10\,\text{m\,s}^{-2}$.

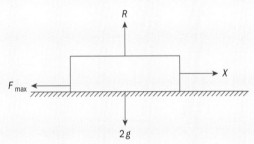

$F_{max} = \mu R$

$= 0.9 \times 2g$

$= 18\,\text{N}$

a) $F_{max} > 10\,\text{N}$, which means that no motion can take place.

b) $F_{max} > 15\,\text{N}$, which means that no motion can take place.

c) $F_{max} < 35\,\text{N}$, which means that motion will take place along the rough surface.

To find its acceleration we will use: resultant force $= ma$.

$(X - F_{max}) = ma$

$(35 - 18) = 2 \times a$

$a = 8.5\,\text{m\,s}^{-2}$

Look back to Chapter 5 where Newton's second law, resultant force $= ma$, was introduced.

Next, in Example 3, we will look at what happens when parallel forces are applied to an object on a rough horizontal surface, and the forces are not parallel to the motion of the object.

Example 3

A 12 kg basket containing fruit and vegetables from the local market is left on a rough horizontal floor. The coefficient of friction between the basket and the rough floor is 0.65. The basket is about to move when a force X is applied at an angle θ to the horizontal. Calculate the magnitude of X when

a) $\theta = 0°$

b) $\theta = 15°$.

Take g as $10 \, \text{m s}^{-2}$.

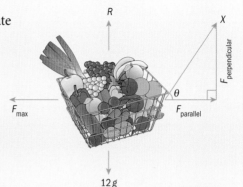

Here we are using F_{parallel} as the component of the applied force parallel to the surface and $F_{\text{perpendicular}}$ as the component of the applied force perpendicular to the surface.

- -

a) Resolving vertically:

$R = mg$

$\quad = 12g = 12 \times 10$

$\quad = 120 \, \text{N}$

In the state of limiting equilibrium, $F_{\text{max}} = X = \mu R$

$X = 0.65 \times 120$

$\quad = 78 \, \text{N}$

This means that for motion to occur, the force being applied must exceed 78 N.

b) From the above diagram we can work out the forces perpendicular and parallel to the floor.

$F_{\text{perpendicular}} = X \sin 15°$

$F_{\text{parallel}} = X \cos 15°$

Resolving vertically:

$R + X \sin 15° = 12g$

$R = 12g - X \sin 15°$

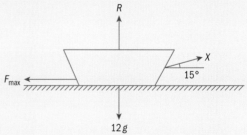

At the time when limiting equilibrium takes place:

$F_{\text{parallel}} = X \cos 15° = F_{\text{max}} = \mu R$

$X \cos 15° = 0.65 \, (12g - X \sin 15°)$

$X(\cos 15° + 0.65 \sin 15°) = 0.65 \times 12g$

$X = 68.8 \, \text{N} \, (3 \text{ s.f.})$

For motion to take place the force must exceed 68.8 N.

Exercise 6.1

The following diagrams show a solid block of granite of mass 700 kg at rest on a rough surface. Given that the coefficient of friction between the block and the surface below it is 0.4, state whether the forces applied are enough to cause it to move.

1.

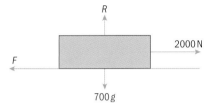

2.

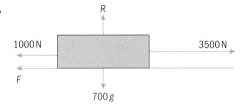

3.

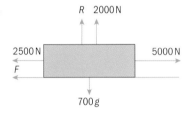

4.

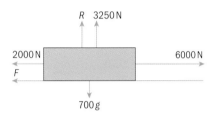

5.

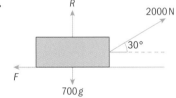

6.

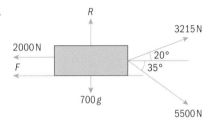

6.2 Rough inclined plane

The diagram shows a body of mass m resting on a rough inclined plane that is at an angle of θ to the horizontal. There is no motion, so resolving at right angles to the plane, $R = mg \cos \theta$.

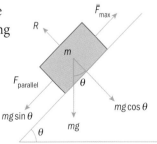

As the parallel force $mg \sin \theta$ is acting down the plane, the frictional force F opposes the direction of this force.

In the system's limiting equilibrium state:

$$F_{max} = \mu R$$
$$= \mu mg \cos \theta$$

Example 4

A sledge of mass 10 kg is about to slip as it rests in limiting equilibrium on a rough inclined plane, at 30° to the horizontal. Find the coefficient of friction between the sledge and the plane.

Take g as $10\,\text{m s}^{-2}$.

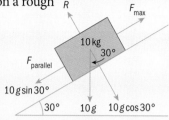

Resolving parallel to the plane:

$10g \sin 30° = \mu R$

Resolving perpendicular to the plane:

$R = 10g \cos 30°$

Substituting this value of R into the equation above we have:

$10g \sin 30° = \mu R = \mu \times 10g \cos 30°$

$\mu = \dfrac{10g \sin 30°}{10g \cos 30°} = \tan 30°$

$\mu = \dfrac{\sqrt{3}}{3} \approx 0.577$

> **Remember:** $\sin 30° = \dfrac{1}{2}$ and $\cos 30° = \dfrac{\sqrt{3}}{2}$, and $\dfrac{1}{\sqrt{3}}$ can also be written as $\dfrac{\sqrt{3}}{3}$.

Example 5

A van is carrying fruit from the local market. It breaks down on a steep hill inclined at 30° to the horizontal. Given that the van and fruit have a mass of 1500 kg and the coefficient of friction between the van's wheels and the surface is 0.56, find the force X parallel to the surface that must be applied to the van to prevent motion down the hill.

Take g as $10\,\text{m s}^{-2}$.

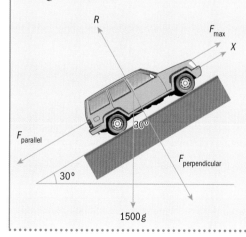

▶ Continued on the next page

As the van is prevented from moving down the hill, frictional force is in the opposite direction, opposing motion.

Resolving perpendicular to the plane:

$R = 1500 g \times \cos 30°$
$\quad = 1500 \times 10 \times \cos 30° = 12\,990.38 \, \text{N}$

Resolving parallel to the plane:

$F_{max} + X = 1500 g \times \sin 30°$

$X = 1500 g \times \sin 30° - \mu R$

$\quad = 1500 g \times \sin 30° - 0.56 \times 12\,990.38$

$\quad = 225 \, \text{N} \, (3 \text{ s.f.})$

Remember: $F_{max} = \mu R$

To prevent the van slipping down, a force of 225 N must be applied.

Example 6

A trailer full of potatoes is at rest on a hill inclined at 55° to the horizontal.

The coefficient of friction between the trailer and the surface is $\dfrac{\sqrt{3}}{2}$.

Given that the trailer with potatoes has a mass of 3500 kg, what is the trailer's acceleration if a force of 47 000 N is applied up the hill along a line of greatest slope?

Take g as $10 \, \text{m s}^{-2}$.

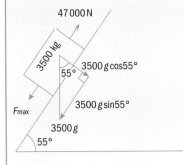

▶ Continued on the next page

Resolving perpendicular to the plane:

$R = 3500\,g \times \cos 55°$
$\quad = 3500 \times 10 \times \cos 55° = 20\,075.18\,\text{N}$

If the trailer is moving up the hill the frictional force F_{max} must be acting down the hill.

$F_{max} = \mu R = \dfrac{\sqrt{3}}{2} \times 20\,075.18$

$\quad = 17\,385.62\,\text{N}$

Also acting down the hill is the parallel force of $3500\,g \sin 55° = 28\,670.32\,\text{N}$.

The total force down the hill is $17\,385.62 + 28\,670.32 = 46\,055.94\,\text{N}$.

Since the force exerted on the trailer going up the hill is greater than the force opposing the trailer, then motion will occur.

Using $F = ma$:

$47\,000 - F_{max} - 3500\,g \sin 55° = 3500a$
$47\,000 - 17385.62 - 28670.32 = 3500a$

So, acceleration $a = 0.270\,\text{m s}^{-2}$.

Remember: Do not round intermediate answers in a multi-step calculation, only the final answer.

Exercise 6.2

1. A sledge of mass 15 kg is released from rest on a rough inclined plane. R is the normal reaction and F is the frictional force exerted on the body by the plane. For each of the following, calculate the magnitude of F and state whether the sledge will remain at rest or will move up or down the plane.

a)
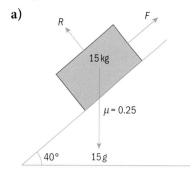

b)
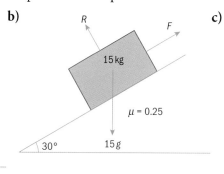

c)
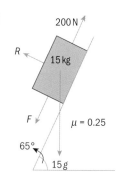

2. A skier of mass 92 kg is just on the point of being pulled up the ski slope by a ski lift. However, the skier is on part of the ground that has just thawed, making it difficult to move. Given that the angle of the slope is 55° to the horizontal, and the coefficient of friction is 0.86, find the magnitude of the force needed to keep the skier on the point of moving up the slope.

3. A crate containing large plastic water bottles is being delivered to houses in and around a city. The first delivery is on a hill of 17° inclined to the horizontal. Given that the van is stationary, pointing down the hill, the mass of the crate and bottles is 230 kg and the coefficient of friction between the crate and the floor of the van is 0.25, what force parallel to the floor of the van must be applied in order for the crate to stop sliding further into the van?

4. A large block is sliding down a hill inclined at 42° to the horizontal with an acceleration of 0.5 m s^{-2}. Given that the block has a mass of 1500 kg, what is the coefficient of friction between the block and the hill?

5. A wooden block of mass 250 kg is being pulled up a hill by a car accelerating at 0.25 m s^{-2}. The hill is inclined at 30° to the horizontal. The force being applied to the wooden block is 2000 N at 35° to the surface, as shown in the diagram. Find the value of μ.

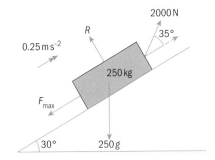

6. The diagram on the right shows a crate of mass 100 kg being pulled up a hill inclined at 30° to the horizontal. One man uses a force of 650 N to pull the crate and another pulls with a force of 175 N. The ropes that they are pulling with are parallel to and inclined at 20° to the surface, respectively. If a force of 100 N is opposing the motion of the crate and is inclined at 45° to the surface, what is the coefficient of friction?

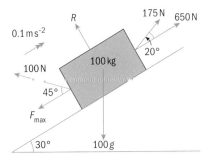

1. A suitcase of mass 5 kg is released from rest at the top of a slope that is fixed at 35° to the horizontal. The coefficient of friction between the suitcase and the surface is 0.15. Ignoring any other resistances, calculate the acceleration of the suitcase as it slides down the slope.

2. A block of mass 2 kg is placed on a rough surface that is inclined at 40° to the horizontal. The block accelerates down the incline at 0.5 m s⁻². Find the coefficient of friction between the block and the surface.

EXAM-STYLE QUESTION

3. A box of mass 20 kg slides down the line of greatest slope of a hill. The hill is inclined at 25° to the horizontal, and the coefficient of friction between the box and the hill is 0.65. Given that the initial speed of the box is 4 m s⁻¹, find the acceleration of the box and the distance the box covers before it stops.

4. A briefcase of mass 5 kg is at rest on a rough horizontal surface. The coefficient of friction between the briefcase and the surface is 0.68. State whether the following horizontal forces being applied are enough to cause it to move.

   a) 20 N   b) 11√3 N   c) 36√6 N.

   Calculate the acceleration that takes place due to its motion.

5. The following diagrams show a block of wood of mass 65 kg at rest on a horizontal surface. *F* is the frictional force and *R* is the normal reaction of the surface to the block. Given that the coefficient of friction between the block and the surface is 0.47, state whether the forces applied are enough to cause it to move.

a)

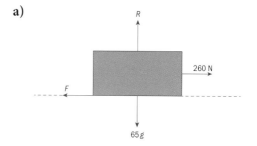

b)

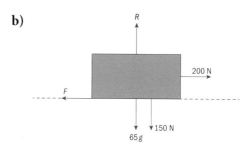

c)

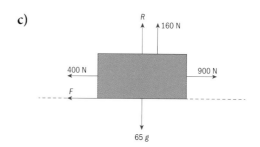

d)

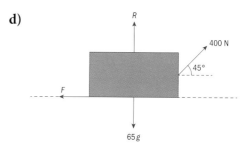

6. A fish tank of mass 60 kg rests in limiting equilibrium on a rough inclined plane at 35° to the horizontal. Find the coefficient of friction between the tank and the plane.

7. A container full of boxes of cereal is sliding down a hill inclined at 25° to the horizontal with an acceleration of 2.5 m s⁻². What is the coefficient of friction between the container and the hill?

EXAM-STYLE QUESTIONS

8. A block of mass 80 kg is moving up a plane that is inclined at 12.6° to the horizontal. The forces acting on it, as well as friction, are 950 N upwards parallel to the plane and 210 N at an angle of 30° to the plane, as shown in the diagram.

   The block accelerates at 1.15 m s^{-2}.

   Determine the coefficient of friction between the block and the plane.

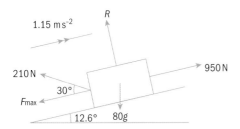

9. A particle of mass 35 kg is in equilibrium on a plane that is inclined at an angle of θ° to the horizontal. The normal reaction force acting on the particle has magnitude 342 N. Find the

   a) value of θ

   b) the least possible value of the coefficient of friction.

10. A suitcase of mass 30 kg rests in limiting equilibrium on a horizontal surface. A force of magnitude 150 N acts on the suitcase at an angle of 25° to the upwards vertical. Determine the coefficient of friction between the suitcase and the ground.

11. A force is pulling a block, of mass 6 kg, along a rough horizontal surface. The pulling force is inclined at 30° above the horizontal and has magnitude 40 N. The coefficient of friction between the block and the surface is 0.65. Find the acceleration of the block.

12. A wooden box of mass 25 kg rests in limiting equilibrium on a rough slope, inclined at 15° to the horizontal. Find the coefficient of friction between the box and the slope.

13. A wooden crate of fish is at rest on a surface that is inclined at 35° to the horizontal. The coefficient of friction between the crate and the surface is $\frac{\sqrt{2}}{6}$. Given that the crate is of mass 250 kg, what is its acceleration if a force of 2000 N is applied up the hill along the line of greatest slope?

Chapter summary

- If resultant force in direction of motion < F_{max} then no motion will take place.
- If resultant force in direction of motion > F_{max} then motion will take place.
- If resultant force in direction of motion = F_{max} then the object is about to slip.
- In the state of limiting equilibrium, $F_{max} = \mu R$.

Maths in real-life

Understanding the Universe

Universal theories are a constant challenge to mathematicians and physicists.

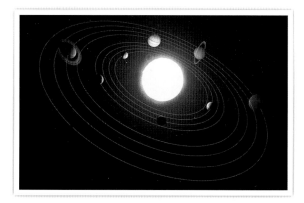

People used to believe that the Earth was the centre of the Universe. In the 16th and 17th centuries, some mathematicians and astronomers developed theories showing that the Earth rotated around the Sun and not vice versa. Copernicus' theories were the first to suggest this.

While Copernicus' theories were essentially correct they were not entirely accurate. This may have been due to the difficulty of collecting observational data when compared with the modern day. Since the 16th century, with the development of technology, there has been significant progress in the development of astronomical theories.

Johannes Kepler published his laws of planetary motion at the very end of the 16th century. However, the forces that dictate the form of the orbits (gravity) were not identified until almost a century later by Sir Isaac Newton.

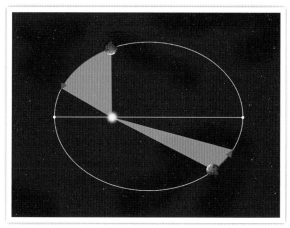

▲ Kepler proposed that the radius vector from Sun to planet sweeps out equal areas in equal time during the elliptical orbit. One consequence of this is that the Earth travels faster when it is close to the Sun than when it is further away.

The theory of planetary motion also governs the behaviour of artificial satellites. These are essential for our modern communications systems to work. Satellites that orbit at about 23 000 miles above the Earth complete one revolution around the Earth in 24 hours. This means that they can stay precisely above a particular location on Earth as it spins on its axis. This is called a geostationary orbit, and it allows a satellite receiver simply to be pointed in one direction to always receive the transmission from that satellite.

▶ One of many communications satellites that we rely on

Newton's theory of gravitation was the basis for all cosmological models for over 200 years until Einstein proposed his theory of relativity in 1905.

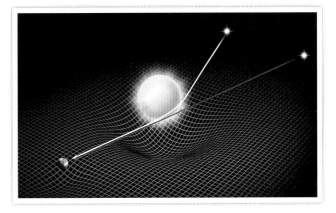

▶ One of the key results of Einstein's theory of relativity is that light will bend around massive objects like stars.

Scientists and mathematicians continue to work to develop more complete theories of how the Universe and its component parts work together. The discovery of the Higgs boson in 2012 caused unheard-of interest among the public in a scientific advance. This discovery earned François Englert and Peter Higgs a Nobel Prize. They had theorised its existence in 1964, but it took 40 years to be discovered. It is a very small particle that provides the evidence to explain why other particles have mass and why they hold together. In succession this explains why we are able to exist. The Higgs boson was a previously missing part of 'The Standard Model' of particle physics. This set of rules lays out our understanding of the fundamental basis of the Universe.

Confirmation of the existence of the Higgs boson will lead to enhanced theories of the nature of the Universe, including, possibly, a better understanding of the mysterious 'dark matter'. Also, the technology that was used to discover the Higgs boson is likely to have applications in other areas of research, such as electronics, computing and medicine.

▼ Some of the detector equipment at the Large Hadron Collider (LHC), CERN, where the Higgs boson was discovered

The Japanese bullet train travels at very high speeds, up to 300 km/h. The train's engine does work and energy is transferred to create the motion. The bullet train is so-called because of its shape and speed. The engineers who designed this train would have made use of the kind of formulae we are learning about to calculate how much work the engine would need to do in order for the train to achieve its high speeds.

Objectives

- Understand the concept of the work done by a force, and calculate the work done by a constant force when its point of application undergoes a displacement not necessarily parallel to the force.
- Understand the concepts of gravitational potential energy and kinetic energy, and use appropriate formulae.
- Understand and use the relationship between the change in energy of a system and the work done by external forces, and use in appropriate cases the principle of conservation of energy.

Before you start

You should know how to:

1. Resolve a force in a given direction.
   e.g. Find the resolved part of the force in the direction of the dotted arrow.

   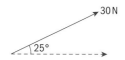

   The resolved part is $30 \cos 25°$
   $= 27.18923361 = 27.2 \text{ N}$ (3 s.f.)

2. Use Newton's first law.
   e.g. A parachutist of mass 85 kg is falling at a constant speed. Find the magnitude of the resistive force experienced by the parachutist.

   Because of Newton's first law, the resultant force on the parachutist is 0.
   Hence, if R is the resistive force, then
   $R - 85g = 0$
   Hence $R = 850 \text{ N}$ (taking g as 10 m s^{-2}).

Skills check:

1. Find the resolved part of each force in the direction of the dotted arrow.

   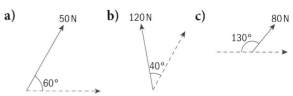

2. **a)** A diver of mass 73 kg is rising from the seabed at a constant speed. Ignoring the resistance of the water, find the upward force acting on the diver.

   b) A lorry is ascending a hill inclined at 2° to the horizontal at a constant speed. The mass of the lorry is 12 000 kg. The resistance to motion is constant and has magnitude 400 N. Find the driving force provided by the lorry's engine.

7.1 Work

When a force moves the point to which it is applied, it is said to do work. Consider a constant force F acting on a particle of mass m. Suppose the particle has an initial speed of $u\,\mathrm{m\,s^{-1}}$ and a final speed of $v\,\mathrm{m\,s^{-1}}$, with the force acting over a distance of s metres.

Then, by Newton's second law, $F = ma$

Since a is a constant, then $\quad v^2 = u^2 + 2as$

Rearranging gives $\quad as = \dfrac{1}{2}v^2 - \dfrac{1}{2}u^2$

Multiplying by m, $\quad mas = \dfrac{1}{2}mv^2 - \dfrac{1}{2}mu^2$

Now, $\quad Fs = mas$

Hence, $\quad Fs = \dfrac{1}{2}mv^2 - \dfrac{1}{2}mu^2 \qquad (1)$

Note: If you were to lift an object, push a heavy box or pedal a bicycle then you would know in each case that you were doing **work**. Work is done whenever a force is applied to an object to change its motion or its position.

> The product of F and s is referred to as the **work done** by the constant force F as the particle moves through a displacement s.

The S.I. unit of work is the **joule** (J), which is the amount of work done when a force of 1 newton moves an object a distance of 1 metre. The joule is named after the English physicist **James Prescott Joule (1818–89)**.

Examination advice
Usually s is used for displacement, but you may sometimes see d used instead.

Did you know?
S.I. is an abbreviation for *Système international d'unités* – the International System of Units.

Example 1

An object of mass 40 kg is pulled a distance of 5 m at constant speed across horizontal rough ground by means of a horizontal rope. The coefficient of friction between the object and the ground is 0.3. Find the work done by each of the forces acting on the object.

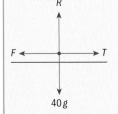

Note: 'By means of' is the same as saying 'with the use of'.

Resolving vertically, we obtain
$R - 40g = 0$
$\qquad R = 400\,\mathrm{N}$
Using $F = \mu R$, where $\mu = 0.3$, then $F = 120\,\mathrm{N}$

▶ Continued on the next page

Resolving horizontally, we obtain

$T - F = 0$

$T = F = 120\,\text{N}$

There is no vertical displacement of the object, so the work done by the weight (400 N) and by R is zero.

The displacement in the direction of T is 5 m, so the work done by the tension = $120 \times 5 = 600\,\text{J}$

The displacement in the direction of F is -5 m, so the work done by the friction = $120 \times -5 = -600\,\text{J}$

Notice the negative work done by friction. We can say the work done by friction is $-600\,\text{J}$, or, more usually, that there is 600 J of work done *against* friction.

It is important to realise that the displacement must take place in the direction of the force. Hence, any forces that are perpendicular to the displacement do no work.

Frequently, the applied force is directed at an angle to the direction that the displacement occurs. For the object in Example 1 the rope used to pull the object may be inclined to the horizontal.

Suppose a force F is applied to an object that is then displaced by a distance s in a direction making an angle θ with the direction of F.

The force F can be resolved into two components: parallel and perpendicular to the direction of the displacement. The perpendicular component, $F\sin\theta$, does no work because there is no displacement in that direction. The parallel component, $F\cos\theta$, is displaced a distance s. Therefore the work done by F is

$$(F\cos\theta) \times s = Fs\cos\theta$$

Example 2

A packing case is pulled along horizontal ground a distance of 6 m by means of a rope inclined at 35° to the horizontal. The tension in the rope is 400 N. Find the work done by the tension.

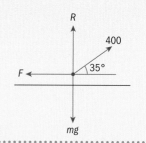

The component of the force in the direction of the motion is $400\cos 35°$.
The displacement in this direction is 6 m.
Hence, work done = $400\cos 35° \times 6 = 1965.964906 = 1970\,\text{J}$ (3 s.f.)

Exercise 7.1

1. A body is pulled a distance of 20 m across a horizontal surface against a resistance of 40 N. If the body moves with constant velocity, find the work done against the resistance.

2. Find the work done by a crane lifting a load of 200 kg at constant speed through a distance of 6.4 m.

3. Find the work done in pulling, at constant speed, a packing case of mass 70 kg a distance of 18 m against a resistance of 150 N on a horizontal surface.

4. A force of 80 N moves an object 15.8 m in the direction of the force. Find the work done by the force.

5. Find the work done by a man of mass 78 kg in climbing vertically up a ladder 5 m high at constant speed.

6. A force of 50 N acts on a block at an angle of 30° above the horizontal. The block moves a horizontal distance of 3 m. Find the work done by the applied force.

7. **Calculate** the work done by a 3 N force, directed at an angle 40° to the upward vertical, to move a box 400 cm across a horizontal floor at constant speed.

8. A woman pushes a package 20 m along level ground at constant speed. The work done by the woman is 160 J. Find the average force resisting the motion.

9. A car is towed at constant speed by means of a tow rope angled at 10° to the horizontal. The work done by the tension in the rope in moving the car 100 m is 2000 J. Find the tension in the rope.

10. A body of mass 8 kg is at rest on a rough horizontal surface. The coefficient of friction between the body and the surface is 0.4. A force of 120 N is applied for a period of 10 s in each of the following cases:

    a)   ●——————→ 120 N   b)   ●⟋⟍ 20° ↗ 120 N

    In each case, find the distance moved by the body and the work done by the 120 N force.

7.2 Kinetic energy

If we refer back to equation (1),

$$Fs = \frac{1}{2}mv^2 - \frac{1}{2}mu^2$$

the left-hand side was the work done by the force F. The right-hand side of the equation has two terms of a similar form.

If an object is moving with a speed v the quantity $\frac{1}{2}mv^2$ is called the **kinetic energy** of the body.

So the kinetic energy (KE) of a body is the energy it possesses because of its motion. Equation (1) tells us that when a force does work on a body so as to increase its speed, then the work done is a measure of the increase in the kinetic energy of the body.

Example 3

A car of mass 1600 kg is travelling along a straight horizontal road at 15 m s^{-1}. The brakes are applied as the car approaches a junction. The car travels 25 m before coming to rest. Find

a) the initial kinetic energy of the car

b) the work done in stopping the car

c) the force applied in stopping the car.

a) The initial kinetic energy of the car $= \frac{1}{2} \times 1600 \times (15)^2 = 180\,000\,\text{J}$

b) The work done in stopping the car = change in kinetic energy = 180 000 J

c) Since work done = force × displacement, force $= \dfrac{180\,000}{25} = 7200\,\text{J}$

Note: Work done and kinetic energy are both measured in joules (J).

Example 4

A body of mass 6 kg increases its energy by 38 J. If its initial speed was 2 m s^{-1}, find its final speed.

Initial kinetic energy $= \frac{1}{2}mv^2$

$$= \frac{1}{2} \times 6 \times (2)^2 = 12\,\text{J}$$

Final kinetic energy = 12 + 38 = 50 J

If the final speed of the body is v, then $50 = \frac{1}{2} \times 6 \times v^2$

$$v = 4.082482905 = 4.08\,\text{m s}^{-1}\ (3\ \text{s.f.})$$

Exercise 7.2

1. Find the kinetic energy of

   a) a body of mass 5 kg moving with speed 4 m s^{-1}

   b) a body of mass 2 kg moving with speed 3 m s^{-1}

   c) a car of mass 1200 kg moving with speed 10 m s^{-1}

   d) a particle of mass 100 g moving with speed 20 m s^{-1}.

2. Find the gain in kinetic energy when

   a) a car of mass 1.4 tonnes increases its speed from $5\,\text{m}\,\text{s}^{-1}$ to $6\,\text{m}\,\text{s}^{-1}$

   b) a body of mass $5\,\text{g}$ increases its speed from $200\,\text{m}\,\text{s}^{-1}$ to $300\,\text{m}\,\text{s}^{-1}$.

3. Find the loss in kinetic energy of

   a) an object of mass $5\,\text{kg}$ that decreases its speed from $3\,\text{m}\,\text{s}^{-1}$ to $2\,\text{m}\,\text{s}^{-1}$

   b) a car of mass $900\,\text{kg}$ that decreases its speed from $14\,\text{m}\,\text{s}^{-1}$ to $10\,\text{m}\,\text{s}^{-1}$.

4. A body of mass $12\,\text{kg}$ is moving at a speed of $4\,\text{m}\,\text{s}^{-1}$. The body's kinetic energy increases by $80\,\text{J}$. Find the final speed of the body.

5. When a squash ball bounces off a wall it loses 20% of its kinetic energy. A squash ball has a mass of $25\,\text{g}$ and hits the wall at $4\,\text{m}\,\text{s}^{-1}$. Find

   a) the kinetic energy of the ball immediately before it hits the wall

   b) the speed of the ball immediately after it rebounds from the wall.

6. A man pushes a car of mass $1200\,\text{kg}$ on a horizontal road from rest. He exerts a horizontal force of $150\,\text{N}$. Ignoring the resistance of the road, find

   a) the work done on the car as it moves $10\,\text{m}$

   b) the speed of the car after $10\,\text{m}$. **Note:** 'Exert' means 'apply'.

7.3 Gravitational potential energy

When a climber scales a rock face, they are doing work against the force of gravity.

Note: The word 'scale' has many mathematical meanings – but here, it means 'climb'.

Suppose we lift an object of mass $15\,\text{kg}$ through a height of $8\,\text{m}$. The work we do against gravity is $15g \times 8 = 1200\,\text{J}$.

If we now allow the object to fall back to its original level, its weight will do $1200\,\text{J}$ of work.

Generalising this to the case of a mass $m\,\text{kg}$, raised vertically through a vertical height of $h\,\text{m}$, the work done against gravity is mass $\times\,g\,\times$ height.

So mgh is the work done against gravity.

If you climb the stairs, then the work done is your weight multiplied by the vertical height gained. In fact the path taken between two points is irrelevant in calculating the work done. The work done is always $mg \times$ (vertical height gained), and is independent of the path taken to gain the height.

By lifting an object we give the object energy. The energy given to it depends on the position of the object in a gravitational field.

> If an object increases its height by a distance h the quantity mgh is the increase in **gravitational potential energy** of the object.

Raising an object increases its gravitational potential energy (GPE), while lowering it decreases its GPE. The amount of energy is simply mgh, where h is the distance above some arbitrary reference point. When an object loses height, this potential energy is converted to kinetic energy.

Example 5

A carriage on a roller coaster ride has a mass of 130 kg. Find the change in potential energy when the carriage descends 12 m.

Change in potential energy $= mgh = 130\,g \times 12 = 15\,600\,\text{J}$

Note: Gravitational potential energy is also measured in joules (J).

Example 6

A climber of mass 75 kg scales a mountain 1.8 km high. Find her gain in potential energy.

Increase in potential energy $= mgh = 75\,g \times 1800 = 1\,350\,000\,\text{J} = 1350\,\text{kJ}$

Note: 1 kJ = 1000 J, and is called a **kilojoule**.

Example 7

A block of mass 2.9 kg slides down the line of greatest slope of a rough inclined plane. The normal reaction between the block and the plane is 2 N.

a) **Show that** if the angle of slope of the plane is θ, then $\cos\theta = \dfrac{21}{29}$.

b) Calculate the change in gravitational potential energy if the block slides a distance of 2.4 m.

a) Resolving forces perpendicular to the plane:

$2.9\,g\cos\theta = 21$

Hence, $\cos\theta = \dfrac{21}{29}$

b) If $\cos\theta = \dfrac{21}{29}$, then

$\sin\theta = \sqrt{1 - \left(\dfrac{21}{29}\right)^2} = \dfrac{20}{29}$

Change in potential energy $= mgh = 2.9\,g \times 2.4 \times \dfrac{20}{29} = 48\,\text{J}$

7.4 Conservation of energy

If, as an object moves, all of its potential energy is converted to kinetic energy, then the situation is called a **conservative system**. If some work is done, other than that done by or against gravity, so that not all the potential energy is converted to kinetic energy, this is a **non-conservative system**.

So the total energy of a system remains constant provided no external work is done and there are no sudden changes in the motion of the system.

> The total energy of a system remains constant provided no external work is done and there are no sudden changes in the motion of the system. This is known as the **principle of conservation of energy**.

Example 8

A ball of mass 0.6 kg is dropped from rest at a height of 10 m above the ground. Neglecting air resistance, find

a) the loss in gravitational potential energy in falling to the ground

b) the gain in kinetic energy at the instant the ball reaches the ground

c) the speed with which the ball hits the ground.

a) The loss in GPE $= mgh = 0.6 \, g \times 10 = 60 \, J$.

b) Because of conservation of energy the kinetic energy gained is equal to the GPE lost. So the gain in kinetic energy is 60 J.

c) The change in kinetic energy is $\frac{1}{2}mv^2 - \frac{1}{2}mu^2$

$$= \frac{1}{2} \times 0.6 \times v^2 - \frac{1}{2} \times 0.6 \times (0)^2 = 60$$

$$v = 14.14213562 = 14.1 \, m \, s^{-1} \, (3 \, s.f.)$$

Exercise 7.4

1. A base jumper with mass 85 kg jumps from the top of a building, 300 m above the ground. He falls with an initial velocity of $4 \, m \, s^{-1}$ towards the ground. He releases his parachute at a point 80 m above the ground. Find

   a) the initial kinetic energy of the jumper

   b) the potential energy lost by the jumper in moving from the top of the building to the point where he releases his parachute

   c) his speed at the instant that he releases his parachute, stating an assumption you have made in modelling this situation.

   > **Did you know?**
   > Base jumping is a sport in which participants jump from a fixed object (such as a building or a cliff) and use a parachute to break their fall.

2. A particle of mass 0.4 kg is projected up a smooth plane inclined at an angle θ to the horizontal, where $\tan \theta = \frac{5}{12}$. The particle moves through a point A at a speed of $12 \, m \, s^{-1}$. The particle continues to move up the line of greatest slope and comes to instantaneous rest at a point B. Find

   a) the height of B above the level of A

   b) the distance AB

   c) the speed of the particle when it returns to A.

3. A parachutist of mass 70 kg jumps from an aeroplane at a height of 1000 m and hits the ground at $6\,\mathrm{m\,s^{-1}}$. Assume that his vertical velocity when he leaves the plane is zero.

Find

   a) the potential energy lost

   b) the work done against the resistive forces during the jump.

4. A body of mass 2 kg is released from rest and falls freely under gravity. Ignoring air resistance, find its speed when it has fallen a distance of 15 m.

5. A body of mass 5 kg is released from rest and falls freely under gravity. Ignoring air resistance, find the distance it has fallen when its speed is $8\,\mathrm{m\,s^{-1}}$.

6. A stone of mass 0.2 kg is dropped down a well. The stone hits the surface of the water with a speed of $16\,\mathrm{m\,s^{-1}}$.

   a) Calculate the kinetic energy of the stone as it hits the water.

   b) Find the height above the water from which the stone was dropped.

   c) When the stone hits the water, it begins to sink vertically and experiences a constant resistance of 18 N. Find the depth the stone has sunk to when the speed of the stone is $4\,\mathrm{m\,s^{-1}}$.

7. A body of mass 4 kg is projected vertically downwards at a speed of $2\,\mathrm{m\,s^{-1}}$. Find the speed of the body as it passes through a point 6 m below the point of projection. Assume there are no resistances to the motion.

8. A and B are two points in a vertical line, with A above B. A body of mass 0.6 kg is released from A and falls vertically, passing through B at a speed of $12\,\mathrm{m\,s^{-1}}$. Find the distance AB. Assume there are no resistances to the motion.

9. A and B are two points in a vertical line, with A above B. A body of mass 0.5 kg falls vertically. It passes through A at a speed of $2\,\mathrm{m\,s^{-1}}$ and passes through B at a speed of $8\,\mathrm{m\,s^{-1}}$. Find the distance AB. Assume there are no resistances to the motion.

10. A and B are two points in a vertical line, with A a distance of 4 m above B. A particle P, of mass m kg, is projected vertically upwards from B at a speed of $15\,\mathrm{m\,s^{-1}}$. Assuming there are no resistances to motion, find

a) the speed of P as it passes through A

b) the speed of P as it passes through A again, travelling downwards

c) the speed of P as it passes through B

d) the height above B of the highest point reached.

11. A smooth slope is inclined at $\tan^{-1}\left(\dfrac{3}{4}\right)$ to the horizontal. A particle of mass 0.4 kg is released from rest at the top of the slope. The particle reaches the bottom of the slope at a speed of 8 m s^{-1}. Find the length of the slope.

12. Point A is at the bottom of a smooth slope that is inclined at an angle θ to the horizontal, where $\tan\theta = \dfrac{7}{24}$. A particle is projected from A at a speed of 16 m s^{-1} up the line of greatest slope of the plane and passes through a point B at a speed of 3 m s^{-1}. Find the distance AB.

7.5 The work–energy principle

The total work done on any system is equal to the total change in energy. This is known as the **work–energy principle**.

As an object moves, if work is done, and so not all of the potential energy is converted to kinetic energy, the system is non-conservative (see Section 7.4). In these situations we can still make use of energy to solve a problem because of the work–energy principle.

Example 9

A particle of mass 4 kg is projected down a plane inclined at 30° to the horizontal at a speed of 1 m s^{-1}. There is a constant resistance of 5 N. Find the speed of the particle after it has travelled 6 m down the plane.

The vertical height lost by the particle is $6\sin 30° = 3$ m.

In moving down the slope the loss in PE of the particle is $mgh = 4g \times 3 = 120$ J.

The gain in KE is $\dfrac{1}{2}mv^2 - \dfrac{1}{2}mu^2 = \dfrac{1}{2} \times 4 \times v^2 - \dfrac{1}{2} \times 4 \times (1)^2 = 2v^2 - 2$.

The work done against the resistance force is $Fs = 5 \times 6 = 30$ J.

Hence, by conservation of energy, the GPE lost is converted into some KE *and* is used to overcome the resistance:

$120 = 2v^2 - 2 + 30$

$v = 6.782329983 = 6.78$ m s^{-1} (3 s.f.)

Example 10

A car of mass 1200 kg has a speed of 26 m s^{-1} at the bottom of a hill inclined at 5° to the horizontal. The car travels up the line of greatest slope of the hill. After a distance of 500 m the car's speed has decreased to 12 m s^{-1}. The resistance to motion is constant and has magnitude 400 N. Find the constant driving force produced by the car's engine.

The vertical height gained by the car is $500 \sin 5° = 43.6$ m (3 s.f.).

In moving up the hill the gain in PE of the car is

$mgh = 1200 \times g \times 43.6 = 522\,934.5$ J

The gain in KE is

$$\frac{1}{2}mv^2 - \frac{1}{2}mu^2 = \frac{1}{2} \times 1200 \times (12)^2 - \frac{1}{2} \times 1200 \times (26)^2$$

$$= \frac{1}{2} \times 1200 \times 144 - \frac{1}{2} \times 1200 \times 676$$

$$= 86\,400 - 405\,600$$

$$= -319\,200 \text{ J}$$

As this value is negative, KE is lost as the car travels up the hill, and the *change* in KE is 319 200 J.

The work done against the resistance force of 400 N is

$(D - 400) \times s = (D - 400) \times 500$

By conservation of energy the KE lost is converted into PE and used to overcome the resistance.

So

$522\,934.5 = 319\,200 + (D - 400) \times 500$

$(D - 400) \times 500 = 203\,734.5$

$D - 400 = 407\,469$

$D = 807.469$

D is used for the driving force.

The driving force $D = 807$ N (3 s.f.).

There are cases where the energy done by a specific force is given. The following example shows how to deal with this type of problem. It cannot be assumed that the force is constant and hence the use of constant acceleration formulae is prohibited.

Example 11

A car of mass 1250 kg travels along a road that has a straight horizontal section *AB* and a straight inclined section *BC*. The length of *BC* is 600 m. The speed of the car at *A*, *B* and *C* is 19 m s^{-1}, 29 m s^{-1} and 19 m s^{-1}, respectively (see diagram).

a) The work done against the resistance to motion of the car, as it travels from *A* to *B*, is 525 kJ. Find the work done by the driving force as the car travels from *A* to *B*.

▶ Continued on the next page

b) As the car travels from B to C, the resistance to motion is 450 N and the work done by the driving force is 370 kJ. Find the height of C above the level of AB.

> **Examination advice**
> It is tempting to use the constant acceleration equations in this question. However, this would require the assumption that the driving force and the resistance are constant, which is not stated in the question. Only the work done by the resistance and by the driving force are given. This is something to be aware of in questions of this type.

a) Gain in KE $= \dfrac{1}{2}mv^2 - \dfrac{1}{2}mu^2 = \dfrac{1}{2} \times 1250 \times 29^2 - \dfrac{1}{2} \times 1250 \times 19^2 = 300\,000$

Work done by driving force = gain in KE + work done against resistance

$$= 300\,000 + 525\,000 = 825\,000 \text{ J} = 825 \text{ kJ}$$

b) Loss in KE $= \dfrac{1}{2}mv^2 - \dfrac{1}{2}mu^2 = \dfrac{1}{2} \times 1250 \times 29^2 - \dfrac{1}{2} \times 1250 \times 19^2 = 300\,000$

Work done against resistance $= 450 \times 600 = 270\,000$ J

Gain in PE $= 1250 \times g \times h = 12\,500h$

Work done by driving force + loss in KE = gain in PE + work done against resistance

$370\,000 + 300\,000 = 12\,500h + 270\,000$

and hence

$h = 32$ m

In the examples considered so far, motion is either vertical or on an inclined plane, in other words it is motion in a straight line. It is also possible to use the work–energy principle to solve problems in situations where the motion is not linear, such as motion on a curved surface.

Example 12

1.5 m

In a playground a small child of mass 20 kg goes down a slide, as shown in the diagram. The slide is 1.5 m high and there is a constant resistance of 10 N between the child and the slide. The total length of the slide is 3.5 m. The child starts from rest at the top of the slide. Find

a) the loss in gravitational energy of the child in sliding to the bottom of the slide

b) the gain in kinetic energy at the instant she reaches the end of the slide

c) her speed at the end of the slide.

▶ Continued on the next page

a) Loss in GPE $= mgh = 20 \times 10 \times 1.5 = 300\,\mathrm{J}$

b) Applying the work–energy principle:

Loss in GPE = gain in KE + work done against resistance

$300 =$ gain in KE $+ 10 \times 3.5$

Gain in KE $= 265\,\mathrm{J}$

> In this question, although the slide is curved, we can still apply the work–energy principle.

c) Gain in KE $= \dfrac{1}{2}mv^2 = \dfrac{1}{2} \times 20v^2 = 265$

$v = 5.15\,\mathrm{m\,s^{-1}}$ (3 s.f.)

Exercise 7.5

1. A and B are two points $8\,\mathrm{m}$ apart on a horizontal smooth surface. A particle of mass $2\,\mathrm{kg}$ is initially at rest at A and is pushed by a force of constant magnitude acting in the direction from A to B. The particle reaches a point B at a speed of $6\,\mathrm{m\,s^{-1}}$. Find the magnitude of the force.

2. A car of mass $1000\,\mathrm{kg}$ descends a hill angled at θ to the horizontal, where $\sin\theta = 0.1$. There is a constant resistance to motion of magnitude $200\,\mathrm{N}$. Find the work done by the brakes in bringing the car to rest from a speed of $9\,\mathrm{m\,s^{-1}}$ in a distance of $50\,\mathrm{m}$. Assuming that the braking force is constant, find the braking force produced by the car.

3. In a downhill ski race, competitors descend from a start point, which is $1800\,\mathrm{m}$ above sea level, to a finish line, which is $1100\,\mathrm{m}$ above sea level. A competitor has a total mass of $85\,\mathrm{kg}$ including equipment. He starts from rest and crosses the finish line at a speed of $12\,\mathrm{m\,s^{-1}}$. Find the work done in overcoming the resistances to his motion.

4. A lorry of mass $5000\,\mathrm{kg}$ accelerates from $5\,\mathrm{m\,s^{-1}}$ to $8\,\mathrm{m\,s^{-1}}$ while covering a distance of $60\,\mathrm{m}$ on a horizontal road. The resistance to motion is constant and of magnitude $250\,\mathrm{N}$. Find the driving force.

5. Find the force needed to accelerate a train of mass 400 tonnes from $12\,\mathrm{m\,s^{-1}}$ to $20\,\mathrm{m\,s^{-1}}$ in a distance of $2\,\mathrm{km}$ along a horizontal track, assuming the resistance to motion is constant and $150\,000\,\mathrm{N}$.

6. A gymnast of mass $60\,\mathrm{kg}$ swings on a rope of length $12\,\mathrm{m}$. Initially the rope makes an angle of $50°$ with the vertical and the gymnast is at rest. Find

a) the decrease in his potential energy when the rope is vertical

b) the speed of the gymnast when the rope is vertical.

7. *A* and *B* are two points 6 m apart on a horizontal smooth surface. A particle of mass 5 kg is initially at rest at *A* and is pushed towards *B* by a constant force of magnitude 12 N. Find the speed of the particle at *B*.

8. A child of mass 28 kg goes down a slide, starting from rest. The total drop in height of the slide is 4.5 m.

    a) If the slide is smooth, find the speed of the child at the bottom of the slide.

    b) In fact the slide is rough, and the child reaches the bottom travelling at a speed of 5 m s⁻¹. Find the work done against friction and the average friction force, given that the total length of the slide is 12 m.

9. A constant force of magnitude 15 N pushes a body of 6 kg in a straight line across a smooth horizontal surface. The body passes through a point *A* at a speed of 3 m s⁻¹ and then through a point *B*, 4 m from *A*. For the motion of the body from *A* to *B*, find

    a) the work done by the 15 N force

    b) the final speed of the body.

10. A skateboarder goes down a ramp formed by the arc of a circle of radius 8 m. The total mass of the skateboarder and her board is 65 kg. She starts from rest at *A*, the top of the ramp, which is at the same height as *O*, the centre of the circle. Find the speed with which she leaves the ramp at *B*, given that there is a constant resistance of 35 N.

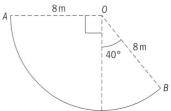

11. A box of mass 4 kg is pushed from rest a distance of 20 m up the line of greatest slope of an inclined plane from a point A to a point B. The height of *B* above the level of *A* is 5 m. While the box is moving, the force in the direction *AB* pushing it is 52 N and the resistance to its motion is 18 N.

    a) Calculate the acceleration of the box up the plane.

    b) Use the work–energy principle to show that the velocity *v* of the box when it reaches *B* is given by $v^2 = 240$.

Summary exercise 7

1. A boy on a sledge, of total mass 30 kg, is pushed from rest with a horizontal force of 50 N against a resistance of 20 N for 16 m along horizontal ground.

   a) Find his speed after moving this distance.

   The pushing force is now removed and he slows down under the same resistance of 20 N.

   b) Find the total distance travelled from the instant the pushing began until he comes to rest.

2. A and B are two points on a line of greatest slope of a smooth inclined plane, with B a vertical distance of 9 m below the level of A. A particle of mass 0.6 kg is projected down the plane from A at a speed of 1.5 m s^{-1}. Find the speed of the particle when it reaches B.

3. A man pulls a block, of mass 25 kg, across a horizontal floor by means of a rope attached to the block and inclined at 20° to the horizontal. The block is pulled a distance of 12 m and the tension in the rope is 80 N.

   a) Find the work done by the man.

   The resistance to the motion of the block is 28 N and the block is initially at rest.

   b) Find the final speed of the block.

4. A box of mass 40 kg is dragged across a horizontal floor by a constant force of magnitude 300 N acting at an angle θ above the horizontal. The total resistance to motion has magnitude 250 N. The box starts from rest at a point A and passes a point B, 20 m from A, at a speed of 1.5 m s^{-1}.

   a) For the box's motion from A to B, find

      i) the increase in the kinetic energy of the box

      ii) the work done against the resistance to motion of the box.

   b) Hence calculate the value of θ.

5. A boy of mass 40 kg is sitting at the top of a water slide at a height of 2.5 m above a swimming pool. The slide is smooth. The boy starts to move down the slide from rest. Ignoring air resistance, find his speed at the instant he enters the pool.

6. A girl of mass 35 kg is at the top of a slide of length 4 m and at a height of 2 m above the ground. She starts to move down the slide from rest. The resistance to motion is constant and of magnitude 20 N. Find her speed at the bottom of the slide.

7. A car of mass 1000 kg descends the line of greatest slope of a hill inclined at an angle α to the horizontal, where $\sin \alpha = 0.2$. The constant resistance to motion has magnitude 300 N. Find the constant breaking force needed to bring the car to rest from 20 m s^{-1} in a distance of 100 m.

8. A skier of mass 70 kg is pulled up a slope, which makes an angle of 15° with the horizontal. The skier is subject to a constant resistance of 50 N. The skier's speed at a point A on the slope is 1 m s^{-1} and, later, at a point B his speed is 2.5 m s^{-1}. The distance AB is 35 m. Find the work done by the pulling force on the skier as he moves from A to B.

9. A girl on a sledge slides down a slope of length 270 m that descends a vertical distance of 60 m. The mass of the girl and sledge in total is 45 kg. The speed of the sledge at the top of the slope is $2 \, \text{m s}^{-1}$ and the speed at the bottom is $5.4 \, \text{m s}^{-1}$. Given that the resistance to motion is constant, find this resistance.

10. A car of mass 1400 kg travels up the line of greatest slope of a hill inclined at 2° to the horizontal. The car passes through a point A at a speed of $5 \, \text{m s}^{-1}$ and through a point B at a speed of $10 \, \text{m s}^{-1}$. Given that the car's engine produces a constant force of 1200 N and the resistance to motion is constant and of magnitude 250 N, find the distance AB.

11. A particle P of mass 0.5 kg is projected at a speed of $v \, \text{m s}^{-1}$ up a rough track in the shape of a quadrant of a circle of radius 2 m, which stands in a vertical plane. The resistance of the track to the motion of the particle is 5 N. The particle comes to rest at a point that is half-way along the track, as shown in the diagram. Calculate

a) the gain in gravitational potential energy of the particle

b) the work done against the resistance

c) the initial speed v of the particle.

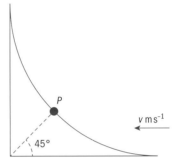

Chapter summary

- Work done by a force F is Fs, where s is the distance moved in the direction of the force.

- Forces perpendicular to the motion do no work.

- Work done by a force F N acting at an angle θ to the direction of motion is $Fs\cos\theta$, where s m is the distance moved in the direction of the force.

- The kinetic energy (KE) of a body of mass m kg moving at a speed of $v \, \text{m s}^{-1}$ is given by $\frac{1}{2}mv^2$.

- The gravitational potential energy (GPE) of a body of mass m kg at a height h above a given reference point is mgh.

- Energy is conserved when no forces other than gravity do work.

- The work–energy principle means that the change in energy is equal to the total work done by the forces acting on the body.

- When specific values of work done by a force are given, then the force cannot be assumed to be constant. The work–energy principle is the only method of solving problems of this type.

- The S.I. unit of energy is the joule (J).

8 Power

A Formula One racing car can develop a great deal of power. A top speed of over $300\,\text{km}\,\text{h}^{-1}$ and an engine generating over $560\,\text{kW}$ of power suggest that the power of the engine is related to the speed of the car. As a racing car travels faster and faster, comparatively more power is required because of the increase in air resistance. In order to build these cars the engineers working on them need to know exactly how fast the car will travel when the engine is producing a certain amount of power.

Objectives

- Use the definition of power as the rate at which a force does work, and use the relationship between power, force and velocity for a force acting in the direction of motion.
- Solve problems involving, for example, the instantaneous acceleration of a car moving up a hill against a resistance.

Before you start

You should know how to:

1. Use Newton's second law.
   e.g. Find the force required to make a car of mass $1000\,\text{kg}$ accelerate by $0.5\,\text{m}\,\text{s}^{-2}$ if the car experiences a resistance of $300\,\text{N}$.

   Using Newton's second law ($F = ma$), the resultant force is mass times acceleration, which gives
   $F - 300 = 1000 \times 0.5$
   Hence $F = 800\,\text{N}$

Skills check:

1. **a)** A bicycle and rider of mass $75\,\text{kg}$ are travelling along a straight horizontal road. The cyclist exerts a forward force of $80\,\text{N}$. The resistance to the motion of the cyclist is $20\,\text{N}$. Find the acceleration of the cyclist.
   b) A car of mass $1200\,\text{kg}$ is travelling down a road inclined at $10°$ to the horizontal. The car experiences a total resistance of $800\,\text{N}$ and is coasting without using the engine. Find the acceleration of the car.

2. Find the work done by a force.

    e.g. A child exerts a horizontal force of 80 N on a sledge carrying a load. Find the work done by the child in moving the sledge 55 m.

Using the definition of work done as force in direction of motion times distance moved ($F \times s$),

work done $= 80 \times 55 = 4400\,\text{J} = 4.4\,\text{kJ}$

2. a) Two people are pushing a car. They each exert a force of 120 N in the direction of motion of the car. Find the work done by the people in moving the car 25 m.

    b) A constant forward force of 8000 N acts on a lorry as the lorry moves forwards on a horizontal road. Find the work done by the force as it moves forwards 60 m.

    c) The work done in moving a train forwards along a horizontal track with no resistance to motion is 40 kJ. If the train moves a distance of 80 m, find the constant driving force of the train's engine.

8.1 Power as the rate of doing work

The work done by a body is important, as we found out in Chapter 7. In some situations it is not only the work done that is significant, but also the time taken to do that work. For example, when a car manufacturer advertises the time taken for their car to reach a given speed they are stating something about the rate at which the engine can work.

The rate at which work is done is called power, which can be expressed in a formula.

$$\text{power} = \frac{\text{work done}}{\text{time taken}}$$

One unit of power is produced when work is done at the rate of one joule per second. This unit is called the watt, W, after **James Watt (1736–1819)**, a Scottish inventor and engineer best known for his work on steam engine development. The watt is a relatively small unit, so it is often useful to use the kilowatt (kW), where 1 kW = 1000 W.

For example, if it takes a car 50 seconds to move 100 m when the average force produced by the engine is 300 N, then the average rate of working or average power is

$$\frac{\text{work done}}{\text{time taken}} = \frac{300 \times 100}{50} = 600\,\text{W}$$

In some cases, when the power is specified, the speed is required at a given time. A car that is moved a distance of s metres in t seconds by a driving force F newtons has

$$\text{power} = \frac{F \times s}{t} = F \times \frac{s}{t}$$

But the quantity $\frac{s}{t}$ is the speed, $v\,\mathrm{m\,s^{-1}}$, of the car.

Hence

$$\boxed{\text{power} = Fv}$$

If the speed is not constant the value of Fv gives the power at the instant when the speed is $v\,\mathrm{m\,s^{-1}}$.

There is obviously a limit to the power that a car or any other vehicle can produce. When the maximum power is attained the speed produced is also a maximum. In this case there is no acceleration possible, and the resultant force is zero.

Example 1

A car moves along a horizontal road against a resistance of 750 N. The maximum power of the car's engine is 12 kW. **Determine** the maximum speed of the car.

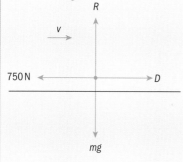

Resolving horizontally: $D - 750 = 0$, so $D = 750$

In this calculation, D is used to represent the driving force. There is no acceleration when at maximum speed, so the forces balance.

To achieve maximum speed, maximum power of 12 000 W needs to be used.

Maximum power = driving force × maximum speed

$12\,000 = 750 \times v$

$v = 16\,\mathrm{m\,s^{-1}}$

Example 2

A mass of 164 kg is raised, by a crane, vertically upwards through a distance of 35 m in 106 seconds. **Calculate** the average power of the crane.

The work done against gravity is $164\,g \times 35 = 57\,400\,\mathrm{J}$.

This work is done in 106 s.

Hence the average power is $\dfrac{57\,400}{106} = 541.509\,434 \approx 542\,\mathrm{W}$ (3 s.f.).

Exercise 8.1

1. Find the average power in raising a body of mass 45 kg at constant speed a vertical distance of 80 m in 20 s ignoring any resistance to motion.

2. Find the average power when lifting a mass of 32 kg vertically at a constant speed of $5\,\mathrm{m\,s^{-1}}$.

3. Find the average rate at which a climber of mass 90 kg must work when climbing a vertical distance at constant speed of 24 m in 2 minutes.

4. In building a section of a wall a man has to lift 400 bricks a vertical distance of 140 cm (assuming constant speed). Each brick has a mass of 1.8 kg, and the man completes the section of wall in 8 minutes. Calculate the man's average rate of working.

5. A car is driven along a straight horizontal road against a resistance to motion of 600 N. Calculate the maximum speed of the car when its engine has a power of

   a) 4 kW   **b)** 6.8 kW   **c)** 9.2 kW.

6. With its engine working at a constant rate of 28 kW the maximum speed a car can attain on level ground is $36\,\mathrm{m\,s^{-1}}$. Find the magnitude of the resistances on the car.

7. A cyclist travels along a straight horizontal road at a constant speed of $9\,\mathrm{m\,s^{-1}}$. The resistance to motion of the cyclist is constant and totals 60 N. Calculate the power generated by the cyclist.

8. A motorcyclist is travelling at a constant speed of $28\,\mathrm{m\,s^{-1}}$ along level ground. The power output of the motorbike engine is 17 500 W. Find the total resistance on the motorcyclist.

9. A cyclist and her bicycle have a total mass of 90 kg. The resistance to her motion is 24 N and the rate at which she is working is 250 W. Determine her maximum speed when

   a) she is travelling on a straight horizontal road

   b) she is travelling up the line of greatest slope of a hill inclined at an angle of 2° to the horizontal

   c) she is travelling down the line of greatest slope of a hill inclined at an angle of 0.5° to the horizontal.

10. With its engines working at a constant power of 350 kW a train of mass 250 000 kg climbs a hill inclined at an angle of 1° to the horizontal at a constant speed of $7\,\mathrm{m\,s^{-1}}$. Find the magnitude of the resistance to motion experienced by the train.

11. A train of mass 400 tonnes is travelling along a straight horizontal track at a constant speed of $25\,\mathrm{m\,s^{-1}}$. The train experiences a constant resistance to motion of magnitude 250 000 N.

   a) Find the rate at which the train's engine is working.

The train now moves up a hill inclined at an angle θ to the horizontal, where $\sin\theta = \dfrac{1}{20}$. The engine continues to work at the same rate, and the magnitude of the non-gravitational resistance remains the same.

b) Find the new constant speed.

12. A car of mass 2400 kg is travelling at a constant speed of $18\,\mathrm{m\,s^{-1}}$ up the line of greatest slope of a road inclined at $8°$ to the horizontal. The non-gravitational resistance to motion is modelled as a single force of magnitude 600 N.

a) Find the power generated by the car's engine during this motion.

When the car passes a point A, travelling at $18\,\mathrm{m\,s^{-1}}$, it begins to coast without any power from the engine until it comes to rest, without braking, a distance $s\,\mathrm{m}$ from A. Find

b) the distance s

c) the time taken for the car to come to rest.

8.2 Acceleration and variable resistance

If, at a particular instant, a vehicle exerts more driving force than the total resistive forces there will be a resultant force in the direction of motion. In this case the vehicle will accelerate. The acceleration can be found by applying Newton's second law.

Be aware that the acceleration will be different at different instants. This is because, if the power remains constant, the vehicle accelerates, changing its speed, and hence the driving force will change. So we can only calculate acceleration at a particular instant in time.

Example 3

A car travels along a horizontal straight road against a constant resistive force of magnitude 275 N. The mass of the car is 1400 kg and its engine is working at a rate of 7.5 kW. Calculate

a) the acceleration at the instant when the car has a speed of $12\,\mathrm{m\,s^{-1}}$

b) the speed of the car at the instant when it is accelerating at a rate of $0.1\,\mathrm{m\,s^{-2}}$ up the line of greatest slope of a hill inclined at an angle of $5°$ to the horizontal.

a)

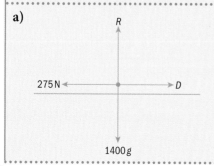

Using $P = Dv$ gives $7500 = D \times 12$, so $D = 625\,\text{N}$.

Resolving horizontally and using $F = ma$ gives $625 - 275 = 1400\,a$.

Hence $a = 0.25\,\text{m s}^{-2}$.

b)

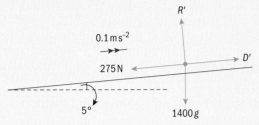

The driving force is $D' = \dfrac{7500}{v}$.

Using $F = ma$ and resolving parallel to the plane gives

$$\frac{7500}{v} - 275 - 1400g\sin 5° = 1400 \times 0.1$$

Hence $v = 4.586649893 \approx 4.59\,\text{m s}^{-1}$.

Example 4

A car of mass $1250\,\text{kg}$ travels on a straight horizontal road. It experiences a resistive force of magnitude $25v\,\text{N}$, where $v\,\text{m s}^{-1}$ is the car's speed. The maximum speed of the car on this road is $60\,\text{m s}^{-1}$. Calculate

a) the car's maximum power

b) the car's maximum possible acceleration when its speed is $30\,\text{m s}^{-1}$.

a) When the car is travelling at its maximum speed, there is no acceleration, and so the driving force of the car, D, must be equal to the resistive force.

$D = 25v$

Power $= (25v) \times v = 25v^2 = 25 \times 60^2 = 90\,000\,\text{W} = 90\,\text{kW}$ ⬅ Since power = force × speed

b)

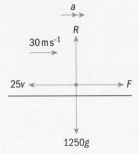

$$\text{Driving force } F = \frac{90\,000}{30} = 3000\,\text{N}$$

Resolving forces horizontally and using Newton's second law gives

$$3000 - (25 \times v) = ma$$

$$3000 - (25 \times 30) = 1250a$$

$$a = 1.8\,\text{m s}^{-2}$$

Exercise 8.2

1. A car of mass 1400 kg is travelling along a straight horizontal road. The resistance to motion of the car is 500 N. At the instant that the car's engine is working at a rate of 8 kW the car has a speed of $10\,\text{m s}^{-1}$. Find the car's acceleration at this instant.

2. A car of mass 800 kg is driven along a horizontal road against a constant resistance to motion of 250 N. With the engine of the car working at a rate of 12 kW, find

    a) the acceleration of the car when its speed is $3\,\text{m s}^{-1}$

    b) the acceleration of the car when its speed is $12\,\text{m s}^{-1}$

    c) the maximum speed of the car.

3. A car of mass 1000 kg is driven along a straight horizontal road against a constant resistance to motion of 300 N. With the engine of the car working at a rate of 8 kW, find

    a) the acceleration of the car when its speed is $4\,\text{m s}^{-1}$

    b) the speed of the car when its acceleration is $2\,\text{m s}^{-2}$

    c) the maximum speed of the car.

4. A train of mass 80 tonnes travels along a level track with its engine developing a constant power of 54 kW.

    a) If the greatest speed the train can reach on this track is $30\,\text{m s}^{-1}$, find the magnitude of the resistance to motion.

    b) Assuming the resistance remains constant and the train's engines still work at 54 kW, find the acceleration of the train when it travels along the track at $15\,\text{m s}^{-1}$.

5. a) A car of mass 850 kg has a maximum speed on a straight horizontal road of $40\,\text{m s}^{-1}$. Determine the maximum power of the engine if the resistance to motion is 280 N.

    b) The car is travelling at $20\,\text{m s}^{-1}$ up a hill, inclined at $\theta°$ to the horizontal, where $\sin\theta = \frac{1}{40}$. The resistance to motion remains unchanged and the engine is exerting maximum power. Find the acceleration of the car.

6. A lorry of mass 8000 kg has a maximum speed of $24\,\mathrm{m\,s^{-1}}$ on a straight horizontal road. The maximum power of the lorry's engine is 30 kW.

    a) Find the total resistance to motion at this speed.

    It is given that the resistance to motion is $kv^2\,\mathrm{N}$, where $v\,\mathrm{m\,s^-}$ is the speed of the lorry and k is a constant.

    b) Find the value of k.

    The lorry now climbs a hill inclined at 2° to the horizontal.

    c) When the lorry is travelling at $12\,\mathrm{m\,s^{-1}}$ and accelerating at a rate of $0.25\,\mathrm{m\,s^{-2}}$, find the power generated by the engine.

7. A car of mass 1200 kg moves up a road inclined at an angle θ to the horizontal, where $\sin\theta = \dfrac{1}{20}$. The car's engine produces a constant power of 30 kW. The car experiences a resistive force of magnitude $kv\,\mathrm{N}$, where k is a constant and v is the car's speed in $\mathrm{m\,s^{-1}}$. At the instant the car has a speed of $10\,\mathrm{m\,s^{-1}}$ its acceleration is $0.8\,\mathrm{m\,s^{-2}}$.

    a) Show that $k = 144$.

    b) Show that V, the maximum speed of the car up this road, satisfies

        $6V^2 + 25V - 1250 = 0$.

        Hence determine the maximum speed of the car on this road.

8. A cyclist and her bicycle have a total mass of 50 kg. She produces a maximum power of 80 W. The resistance to the motion of the cyclist is proportional to her speed. On a straight horizontal road she can travel at a maximum of $10\,\mathrm{m\,s^{-1}}$. On a hill inclined at an angle α to the horizontal, she can freewheel down the hill with a maximum speed of $15\,\mathrm{m\,s^{-1}}$. Find

    a) the value of α

    b) the maximum speed at which she can go up the same hill.

9. A car's engine is working with maximum power $P\,\mathrm{W}$. The car has a mass of 1000 kg and is travelling along a straight level road and experiences a resistance of $R\,\mathrm{N}$. At one instant it is travelling at a speed of $4\,\mathrm{m\,s^{-1}}$ with an acceleration of $2.5\,\mathrm{m\,s^{-2}}$. At a later time, it is travelling at a speed of $8\,\mathrm{m\,s^{-1}}$ with an acceleration of $0.5\,\mathrm{m\,s^{-2}}$. Find the values of P and R.

10. A car's engine has a power output of 50 kW and the car has a mass of 1000 kg. On a straight horizontal road the car has a greatest speed of 40 m s⁻¹. The resistance to the car's speed is variable and has magnitude kv N, where k is a constant and v is the car's speed in m s⁻¹.

a) Evaluate k.

The car now travels on a road inclined at 5° to the horizontal. Determine its maximum speed when

b) going up the hill

c) going down the hill.

Summary exercise 8

1. Find the average rate at which a climber, of mass 75 kg, must work when climbing a vertical distance of 40 m in 150 seconds at constant speed, ignoring air resistance.

2. A crane lifts a block of mass 50 kg to a height of 12 m at a constant speed of 0.6 m s⁻¹. Find the power required.

3. A car has a maximum speed of 50 m s⁻¹ on a straight horizontal road and a maximum power output of 40 kW. The resistive force, R N at a speed of v m s⁻¹, is given by $R = kv$. Find

   a) the value of k

   b) the resistance when the car's speed is 20 m s⁻¹

   c) the power needed to travel at a constant speed of 20 m s⁻¹ along a straight horizontal road.

EXAM-STYLE QUESTION
4. a) The power produced by the engine of a car, as it travels on a straight horizontal road at a constant speed of 60 m s⁻¹, is 30 kW. Find the resistance to motion of the car.

   b) The car has a mass of 1200 kg and is ascending a hill inclined at 4° to the horizontal. Given that the rate at which the car's engine is working and the resistance to motion are unchanged, determine the maximum steady speed on the hill.

5. A train of mass 20 tonnes produces a maximum power of 2000 kW on a horizontal track. The resistance to the motion of the train is 40 kN.

   a) Find the maximum speed of the train.

   b) Find the acceleration of the train at the instant it is moving at a speed of 25 m s⁻¹. Assume the train is working at maximum power.

EXAM-STYLE QUESTION
6. A car has a mass of 800 kg and a maximum power of P W. The car has a top speed of 45 m s⁻¹ on a straight horizontal road and a top speed of 24 m s⁻¹ up a hill inclined at an angle θ to the horizontal, where $\sin \theta = 0.4$. Given that the resistance to motion is constant and has magnitude R N, state two equations connecting P and R. Hence find the values of P and R.

7. The forces resisting the motion of a car are constant at all speeds and total 480 N. When the engine is working at a rate of P kW the maximum speed of the car on a straight horizontal road is $36\,\mathrm{m\,s^{-1}}$.

   a) Find the value of P.

   The car is moving at this maximum speed when the power of the engine is suddenly increased to $(P + 20)$ kW, and the resulting initial acceleration of the car is $0.25\,\mathrm{m\,s^{-2}}$.

   b) Find the mass of the car.

   The car travels down a straight road inclined at $6°$ to the horizontal at a constant speed of $12\,\mathrm{m\,s^{-1}}$ with the brakes working at a rate of Q kW to provide a constant braking force.

   c) Find the value of Q.

EXAM-STYLE QUESTION

8. The total mass of a motorbike and its rider is 300 kg. The maximum power of the motorbike's engine is P kW. When the speed of the motorbike is $v\,\mathrm{m\,s^{-1}}$ the resistance to motion is kv N, where k is a constant. The motorbike has a maximum steady speed of $20\,\mathrm{m\,s^{-1}}$ when ascending a hill inclined at an angle $\sin^{-1}\dfrac{1}{10}$ to the horizontal.

   a) Verify that $5P = 2k + 30$.

   The maximum steady speed going down the same hill is $30\,\mathrm{m\,s^{-1}}$.

   b) Derive another equation relating k and P and hence find the values of k and P.

   c) Determine the maximum steady speed of the motorbike on a straight horizontal road.

9. A car of mass 800 kg has a maximum speed of $28\,\mathrm{m\,s^{-1}}$ when travelling up the line of greatest slope of a hill against a resistance of 500 N. The hill is inclined at an angle θ to the horizontal, where $\sin\theta = \dfrac{1}{40}$. Find the power output of the car's engine.

10. A car of mass 1.4 tonnes moves at a constant speed of $6\,\mathrm{ms^{-1}}$ up a line of greatest slope of a hill inclined at an angle θ to the horizontal, where $\sin\theta = \dfrac{1}{7}$. Given that the engine is working at a rate of 18 kW, find the resistance to the motion of the car.

Chapter summary

- Power is the rate at which work is done and is given by $P = \dfrac{\text{work done}}{\text{time taken}}$.
- The power produced by a force F N on a vehicle moving at a speed of $v\,\mathrm{m\,s^{-1}}$ is given by $P = Fv$.
- The S.I. unit of power is the watt (W).

Momentum is the quantity of motion of a moving body. In a basic sense, the more momentum a moving object has, the harder it is to stop. Momentum can be defined as 'mass in motion'. All objects have mass; so if an object is moving, then it has momentum.

Objectives

- Use the definition of linear momentum and show understanding of its vector nature.
- Use conservation of linear momentum to solve problems that may be modelled as the direct impact of two bodies.

Before you start

You should know how to:

1. Solve linear equations.

   e.g. Solve $12 = -6 + 4v$

   $12 + 6 = 4v$

   $18 = 4v$

   $v = 4.5$

2. Calculate the kinetic energy of a body in motion.

   e.g. Calculate the kinetic energy of a particle of mass 3 kg and speed 4 m s⁻¹.

   $KE = \dfrac{1}{2}mv^2 = \dfrac{1}{2} \times 3 \times 4^2 = 24\,J$

Skills check:

1. Solve these linear equations.

   a) $3v + 7 = 19$

   b) $11 - 4v = 5$

   c) $4m - 11 = -5 + 2m$

2. **a)** Calculate the kinetic energy of the following:

   i) a particle of mass 5 kg moving at a speed of 3 m s⁻¹

   ii) a car of mass 1200 kg moving at a speed of 10 m s⁻¹.

   b) Find the change in kinetic energy of a particle of mass 0.6 kg that has its speed increased from 2 m s⁻¹ to 5 m s⁻¹.

9.1 Momentum

We know that a force is needed to change the velocity of an object. The force required to change the object's velocity is dependent on the mass of the object. The precise relationship between force, mass and velocity can be established by combining Newton's second law with one of the equations of motion for constant acceleration.

Consider a constant force F N that acts for a time t seconds on a body of mass m kg in the body's direction of motion. The force causes the body's velocity to increase from u m s^{-1} to v m s^{-1}. As the force is constant the acceleration a m s^{-2} it produces is constant also.

Note: Newton's second law was considered in Section 5.1, and the equations for constant acceleration in Section 2.1.

Using Newton's second law, $F = ma$, and the equation of motion $v = u + at$ gives

$$F = m\left(\frac{v-u}{t}\right)$$

and hence

$$Ft = mv - mu$$

Note: The quantity Ft is called the 'impulse' of the force. For the purposes of the examination, knowledge and understanding of impulse is not required.

The right-hand side of the above equation is $mv - mu$, which is the change in the value of (mass × velocity). This product of the mass and the velocity of a body is called its **momentum**.

$$\text{momentum} = mv$$

Since momentum is a scalar multiple of velocity, which is a vector, then it follows that momentum is also a vector. The units used for momentum are those of Ft, that is, newton seconds (N s).

Note: You need to consider only motion in one dimension, that is, in a straight line.

Example 1

A particle of mass 4 kg has an initial velocity of 5 m s^{-1}. Find

a) the momentum of the particle

b) the magnitude of the change in momentum if the velocity of the particle increases to 12 m s^{-1}.

· ·

a) $mv = 4 \times 5 = 20$

The initial momentum of the particle is 20 N s.

b) $mv = 4 \times 12 = 48$

The final momentum is 48 N s.

The change in momentum = 48 − 20 = 28 N s.

Example 2

A particle of mass 2.5 kg has an initial velocity of $3\,\mathrm{m\,s^{-1}}$. Find the magnitude of the change in momentum of the particle if

a) the final speed of the particle is $5\,\mathrm{m\,s^{-1}}$ with the direction of motion unchanged

b) the final speed of the particle is $5\,\mathrm{m\,s^{-1}}$ with the direction of motion reversed.

- -

a) Initial momentum $= mv = 2.5 \times 3 = 7.5\,\mathrm{N\,s}$

　　Final momentum $= mv = 2.5 \times 5 = 12.5\,\mathrm{N\,s}$

　　Change in momentum $= 12.5 - 7.5 = 5.0\,\mathrm{N\,s}$

b) Initial momentum $= mv = 2.5 \times 3 = 7.5\,\mathrm{N\,s}$

　　Final momentum $= mv = 2.5 \times (-5) = -12.5\,\mathrm{N\,s}$

　　Change in momentum $= -12.5 - 7.5 = -19.5\,\mathrm{N\,s}$

　　Magnitude of change in momentum $= 19.5\,\mathrm{N\,s}$

> Take the original direction of motion as positive. Then the final velocity is negative.

Exercise 9.1

1. Find the magnitude of the momentum of

   a) a car of mass 1200 kg moving with a speed of $20\,\mathrm{m\,s^{-1}}$

   b) a ball of mass 300 g moving with a speed of $8\,\mathrm{m\,s^{-1}}$

   c) a child of mass 40 kg running with a speed of $3\,\mathrm{m\,s^{-1}}$

   d) a train of mass 230 tonnes travelling at $48\,\mathrm{m\,s^{-1}}$

   e) a lorry of mass 3000 kg moving at $14\,\mathrm{m\,s^{-1}}$.

2. A squash ball of mass 20 g is given a speed of $16\,\mathrm{m\,s^{-1}}$. **Calculate** the momentum of the squash ball.

3. A frog of mass 28 g jumps with an initial speed of $8\,\mathrm{m\,s^{-1}}$. Find the initial momentum of the frog.

4. A lorry of mass 6 tonnes reduces its speed from $15\,\mathrm{m\,s^{-1}}$ to $8\,\mathrm{m\,s^{-1}}$. Calculate the change in momentum of the lorry.

5. A cricket ball of mass 160 g is bowled and reaches the bat with a speed of $18\,\mathrm{m\,s^{-1}}$. The ball is hit directly back to the bowler with a speed of $25\,\mathrm{m\,s^{-1}}$. Find the magnitude of the change in momentum of the ball.

6. A ball of mass 300 g is dropped onto a floor from a height of 2 m and rebounds to a height of 1.4 m. Calculate the change in momentum when the ball hits the floor.

9.2 Collisions

Note: Newton's third law was considered in Section 5.1.

When two bodies are in contact, according to Newton's third law they exert equal and opposite forces (F and $-F$) on each other. Whether the bodies are in contact for a long or a short time the time that each is in contact with the other (t) is the same. Hence, if no external forces act on the bodies the change in momentum of each must be equal and opposite. (Remember from Section 9.1 that $Ft = mv - mu$.)

Note: Two bodies in contact can be said to exert equal and opposite impulses on each other.

▲ It was the work of Newton, in particular his third law, that made us realise that objects in collision transfer momentum from one to the other. Newton's cradle is an example of the conservation of momentum.

Consider bodies A and B, of masses m_A and m_B, which collide. Suppose their velocities before impact are u_A and u_B, and after impact are v_A and v_B.

before collision   after collision

u_A	u_B		v_A	v_B
(A)→	(B)→		(A)→	(B)→
m_A	m_B		m_A	m_B

The change in momentum of A is $m_A v_A - m_A u_A$.

The change in momentum of B is $m_B v_B - m_B u_B$.

Note: In all cases we model the bodies by equally sized spheres and assume that the collision is direct, along the line joining the centres of the spheres.

The change in momentum of each is equal and opposite, so

$$m_A v_A - m_A u_A = -(m_B v_B - m_B u_B)$$

and hence

$$m_A u_A + m_B u_B = m_A v_A + m_B v_B$$

This equation states that

> total momentum before impact = total momentum after impact

This result is known as the **principle of conservation of linear momentum**. It applies for all collisions, provided no external force acts.

Example 3

A particle of mass 2 kg travels at a speed of 5 m s^{-1}. It collides with a stationary particle of mass 8 kg. After the impact the 2 kg mass has a speed of 3 m s^{-1} and its direction of motion is reversed. Find the speed of the 8 kg mass after the impact.

Momentum before collision = $2 \times 5 + 8 \times 0 = 10$

Momentum after collision = $2 \times (-3) + 8 \times v$

> The direction of the 2 kg mass reverses.

$$= -6 + 8v$$

By the principle of conservation of momentum:

$$10 = -6 + 8v$$

$$v = 2 \text{ m s}^{-1}$$

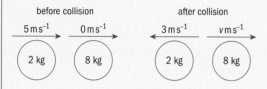

before collision

5 m s^{-1} 0 m s^{-1}

2 kg   8 kg

after collision

3 m s^{-1} v m s^{-1}

2 kg   8 kg

> Drawing a sketch of the situation immediately before and immediately after the collision greatly aids understanding of the situation. It allows any variables introduced to be clearly defined, particularly the direction of a velocity.

Example 4

Two particles, A and B, of masses 2 kg and 3 kg, respectively, are moving towards each other in the same straight line with speeds u m s^{-1} and $2u$ m s^{-1}, respectively. The two particles collide and coalesce. They continue to move in the initial direction of B before the impact, at a speed of 4 m s^{-1}. Calculate u.

> Note: 'coalesce' means join together to form one object.

Momentum before collision = $2 \times u + 3 \times (-2u) = -4u$

Momentum after collision = $5 \times (-4) = -20$

By the principle of conservation of momentum

$$-4u = -20$$

$$u = 5$$

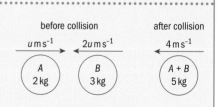

before collision

u m s^{-1} $2u$ m s^{-1}

A   B
2 kg   3 kg

after collision

4 m s^{-1}

A + B
5 kg

Example 5

A lorry of mass 3 tonnes is moving at a constant speed of $4\,\mathrm{m\,s}^{-1}$ when it collides with another lorry, of mass 5 tonnes, moving at a speed of $2\,\mathrm{m\,s}^{-1}$ in the same direction. The speed of the 5-tonne truck is increased to $5\,\mathrm{m\,s}^{-1}$ by the collision. **Show that** the speed of the 3-tonne lorry is $1\,\mathrm{m\,s}^{-1}$ after the collision and find its direction of motion.

We model the two lorries as particles and sketch 'before' and 'after' diagrams.

The final direction of the 3-tonne lorry is unknown. But for calculation purposes we define the final velocity v on the diagram to be to the right, that is, in the positive direction.

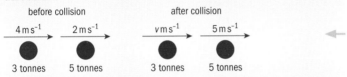

Note: In momentum problems, real objects are modelled as particles, so that the impact forces can be assumed to be directly along the line of motion.

Momentum before collision $= 3000 \times 4 + 5000 \times 2 = 22\,000$

Momentum after collision $= 3000 \times v + 5000 \times 5$

$$= 3000v + 25\,000$$

Note: If the value of v is by calculation shown to be positive, then the direction assumed is correct. If the calculated value of v is negative, then the final direction of motion of the 3-tonne lorry is to the left.

By the principle of conservation of momentum:

$3000v + 25\,000 = 22\,000$

$$v = -1$$

The value of v we get from calculation is negative, which shows that the assumption that the lorry was moving to the right after the collision was incorrect: it was moving to the left.

Hence the speed of the 3-tonne lorry after the collision is $1\,\mathrm{m\,s}^{-1}$.

Its direction of motion is reversed.

Exercise 9.2

1. The following diagrams show the situation before and after a collision between two bodies, A and B, moving along the same straight line on a smooth horizontal surface. Find the missing speed v in each case.

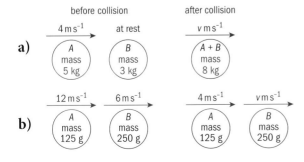

Note: When the surface is said to be smooth there is no loss of kinetic energy due to friction, so the bodies are moving with the given speeds when they collide.

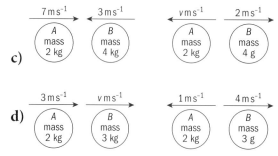

c)

d)

2. Two spheres, *A* and *B*, of masses 250 g and 450 g, respectively, are travelling towards each other along a smooth horizontal surface with speeds of 4 m s^{-1} and 2 m s^{-1}, respectively. After they collide the direction of motion of *B* is reversed and it now has a speed of 1 m s^{-1}. Find the speed of *A* and its direction of motion after the collision.

3. A snooker ball collides directly with an identical ball that is initially at rest. The first ball has its speed reduced from 1.5 m s^{-1} to 0.2 m s^{-1} and continues to move in the same direction. Show that the speed of the second ball after the collision is 1.3 m s^{-1}.

4. A lorry of mass 9 tonnes is travelling at 10 m s^{-1} when it hits a stationary car of mass 1200 kg. The two vehicles move off together after the collision. Modelling the two vehicles as particles, find their initial combined speed.

5. Two bodies, *A* and *B*, of masses 4 kg and *m* kg, respectively, are travelling in the same direction in the same straight line. *A* is travelling at a speed of 5 m s^{-1} and *B* is travelling at a speed of 3 m s^{-1} before they collide. After the collision, *A* and *B* continue to travel in the same direction at speeds of 2 m s^{-1} and 4 m s^{-1}, respectively. Find the value of *m*.

6. Two particles, *A* and *B*, have masses 2 kg and 5 kg, respectively. Immediately before the collision, *A* has a speed of 6 m s^{-1} and *B* has a speed of 3 m s^{-1}, in the same straight line. They collide and coalesce. Find the speed of the combined particle immediately after the collision if

   a) they are initially travelling in the same direction

   b) they are initially travelling in opposite directions.

7. A sledgehammer of mass 6 kg, moving at 24 m s^{-1}, strikes the top of a post of mass 2 kg and does not rebound. Find the common speed of the hammer and post immediately after impact.

8. Two small balls, P and Q, have masses 0.5 kg and 0.2 kg, respectively. They are moving towards each other on a smooth horizontal surface when they collide. Immediately before the collision the speed of P is 8 m s^{-1} and the speed of Q is 2 m s^{-1}. Immediately after the collision the direction of motion of P is unchanged and the speed of Q is double the speed of P. Find

   a) the speed of P immediately after the collision

   b) the change in the momentum of Q.

9. Particles A, B and C have masses 0.2 kg, 0.5 kg and m kg, respectively. The particles lie, in the order ABC, in a straight line on a smooth horizontal surface. Particle B is at rest and particles A and C are moving towards B. Particle A has a speed of 4 m s^{-1} and particle C has a speed of 2 m s^{-1}.

   a) A collides with B. After the collision, A continues to move in the same direction as before the collision. The speed of A is now 0.3 m s^{-1}. Find the speed with which B starts to move.

   b) B and C now collide, after which they both move away from A with speeds of 0.4 m s^{-1} and 0.5 m s^{-1}, respectively. Find the value of m.

10. Two spheres, A and B, have masses 0.1 kg and 0.3 kg, respectively. They are travelling towards each other. The speed of A is 5 m s^{-1} and the speed of B is 2 m s^{-1}. After they collide, A has a speed of 2.5 m s^{-1} and its direction of motion is reversed.

   a) Find the speed and direction of motion of B after the collision.

   b) Find the loss of kinetic energy due to the collision.

Hint: Look back to Section 7.2 for a reminder of kinetic energy calculations.

Summary exercise 9

1. Two particles, P and Q, are projected towards each other on a smooth horizontal surface. P has mass 0.6 kg and initial speed 2.8 m s^{-1}, and Q has mass 0.8 kg and initial speed 1.2 m s^{-1}. After a collision between P and Q the speed of P is 0.1 m s^{-1} and the direction of its motion is reversed.

   a) Calculate the change in momentum of P.

   b) Find the speed and direction of motion of Q after the collision.

2. Two particles of masses 50 g and 80 g are moving towards each other on a smooth horizontal surface. The initial speed of the 50 g mass is 3.9 m s^{-1} and that of the 80 g mass is 3.25 m s^{-1}. The particles collide and coalesce. Find the speed and direction of motion of the combined particle.

: EXAM-STYLE QUESTIONS

3. Each of two wagons has an unloaded mass of 1500 kg. One of the wagons carries a load of mass m kg and the other wagon is unloaded. The wagons are moving towards each other on the same rails, each with a speed of 2 m s^{-1}, when they collide. Immediately after the collision the loaded wagon is at rest and the speed of the unloaded wagon is 3 m s^{-1}. Find the value of m.

4. A spacecraft of mass 40 000 kg docks with a space station of mass 160 000 kg. The spacecraft is travelling at 202 m s^{-1} immediately before docking takes place and the space station is travelling at 200 m s^{-1}. The docking is modelled by two particles moving in the same straight line that collide and coalesce.

   a) Calculate the exact speed of the spacecraft and space station after the docking.

   b) Calculate the total loss in kinetic energy during the docking.

5. Two spheres, P and Q, have masses 0.4 kg and 0.3 kg, respectively. The spheres are moving directly towards each other on a smooth horizontal surface and collide. Immediately before the collision, P has a speed of 6 m s^{-1} and Q has a speed of 4 m s^{-1}. Immediately after the collision the spheres move away from each other, P at a speed of v m s^{-1} and Q at a speed of $(5 - v)$ m s^{-1}. Find the value of v.

: EXAM-STYLE QUESTION

6. A railway wagon A of mass 1200 kg, moving at a speed of 4 m s^{-1}, collides with a railway wagon B, which has mass 1800 kg and is moving towards A at a speed of 2 m s^{-1}. Immediately after the collision the speeds of A and B are equal.

   a) Given that the two wagons are moving in the same direction after the collision, find their common speed. **Determine** which wagon has changed its direction of motion.

   b) It is given instead that A and B are moving with equal speeds in opposite directions after the collision.

      i) Calculate the speed of the wagons after the collision.

      ii) Calculate the change in the momentum of A as a result of the collision.

7. A toy car of mass 240 g collides directly with a stationary toy lorry of mass 360 g. The car's speed is reduced by 3 m s^{-1}. Find the speed of the lorry after the collision.

8. Two particles, of masses 0.2 kg and m kg, are moving towards each other and collide directly. Immediately before the collision the 0.2 kg particle has a speed of $4\,\mathrm{m\,s^{-1}}$ and the m kg particle has a speed of $2\,\mathrm{m\,s^{-1}}$.

   a) Given that both particles are brought to rest by the collision, find the value of m.

   b) Given instead that after the collision both particles move at a speed of $0.5\,\mathrm{m\,s^{-1}}$, find all the possible values of m.

9. Two particles, A and B, of masses 2 kg and 1 kg, respectively, are initially moving towards each other on a smooth horizontal surface. Initially, the speed of A is $3\,\mathrm{m\,s^{-1}}$ and the speed of B is $1\,\mathrm{m\,s^{-1}}$. The particles collide. The direction of motion of A remains unchanged and the direction of motion of B is reversed. The loss of kinetic energy due to the collision is 5.25 J. Find the speeds of the particles after the collision.

10. Three smooth spheres, P, Q and R, of equal radii and of masses 5 kg, 4 kg and 6 kg, respectively, lie in that order in a straight line on a smooth horizontal plane. Initially, Q and R are at rest and P is moving towards Q at a speed of $9\,\mathrm{m\,s^{-1}}$. After colliding with Q, sphere P continues to move in the same direction but at a speed of $2\,\mathrm{m\,s^{-1}}$.

    a) Find the speed of Q after this collision.

    Sphere Q collides with sphere R. In this collision these two spheres coalesce to form an object S.

    b) Find the speed of S after this collision.

    c) Show that the total loss of kinetic energy in the system due to the two collisions is 131.25 J.

11. Two particles, A and B, are travelling in the same direction at different but constant speeds along a straight line when they

collide. Particle A has mass 1.5 kg and speed $6\,\mathrm{m\,s^{-1}}$. Particle B has mass 2.5 kg and speed $2\,\mathrm{m\,s^{-1}}$. The particles coalesce during the collision. Find the speed of the combined particle after the collision.

12. Two model cars, A and B, have masses 250 grams and m grams, respectively. The cars move towards each other in a straight line on a horizontal table. They collide directly when the speed of A is $4\,\mathrm{m\,s^{-1}}$ and the speed of B is $2\,\mathrm{m\,s^{-1}}$. As a result of the collision the speed of A is reduced to $2\,\mathrm{m\,s^{-1}}$ and it continues to move in the same direction as before the collision. The direction of B's motion is reversed and its speed immediately after the collision is $3\,\mathrm{m\,s^{-1}}$. Find the value of m.

13. A particle P moves across a smooth horizontal surface in a straight line. P has mass 2 kg and speed $6\,\mathrm{m\,s^{-1}}$. A particle Q, of mass 3 kg, is at rest on the surface. Particle P collides with particle Q.

    a) Given that after the collision, P is at rest and Q moves away from P, find the speed of Q.

    b) Given instead that after the collision, P and Q move away from each other with the same speed $v\,\mathrm{m\,s^{-1}}$, find v.

14. Two particles, P and Q, have masses 1.2 kg and 0.4 kg, respectively. They are moving towards each other on a horizontal surface when they collide directly. Immediately before the collision the speed of P is $2.5\,\mathrm{m\,s^{-1}}$ and the speed of Q is $1.5\,\mathrm{m\,s^{-1}}$. Immediately after the collision, P and Q move in the same direction and the speed of Q is three times the speed of P.

    a) Find the speed of P immediately after the collision.

    b) Find the change in momentum of P.

c) Find the total loss in kinetic energy due to the collision.

15. Two railway coaches, A and B, of masses 800 kg and m kg, respectively, are moving in opposite directions towards each other when they collide. Immediately before the collision the speed of A is 5 m s^{-1} and the speed of B is 2.5 m s^{-1}. Immediately after the collision the coaches join together and move with the same speed of 0.5 m s^{-1}. The direction of motion of A is unchanged by the collision.

    a) Find the value of m.

    b) Find the change in momentum of B.

16. Particles A and B, with masses 0.5 kg and m kg, respectively, are moving on a smooth horizontal table in opposite directions and collide. Immediately before the collision the speed of A is 4 m s^{-1} and the speed of B is 2 m s^{-1}. Due to the collision, A's direction of motion is reversed, and the momentum of A changes by 2.8 N s.

    a) Find the speed of A immediately after the collision.

    b) Given that the speed of B immediately after the collision is 1 m s^{-1}, find the two possible values of m.

17. Two particles, P and Q, of masses $4m$ kg and m kg, respectively, are moving towards each other on a horizontal surface. Immediately before they collide, P has a speed of 2 m s^{-1} and Q has a speed of 11 m s^{-1}. Immediately after the impact the direction of motion of both particles has been reversed and they are both travelling with the same speed v m s^{-1}.

    a) Show that $v = 1$.

    The change in momentum of A during the collision is -18 N s.

    b) Find the value of m.

18.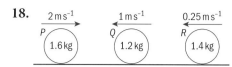

    Three particles, P, Q and R, have masses 1.6 kg, 1.2 kg and 1.4 kg, respectively. The particles are moving in a straight line on a smooth horizontal table, with Q between P and R. The particle P is moving towards Q at a speed of 2 m s^{-1} and the particles Q and R are moving towards P at speeds of 1 m s^{-1} and 0.25 m s^{-1}, respectively.

    a) P collides with Q. As a result of this collision the direction of motion of Q is reversed and its speed remains 1 m s^{-1}. Find the speed of P after the collision.

    b) Q collides with R.

        i) Find the total momentum of Q and R in the direction of Q's motion immediately before the collision takes place, and **verify** that the direction of motion of R is reversed as a result of this collision.

        ii) Given that Q is brought to rest by this collision, find the speed of R immediately after this collision.

19. Two particles, A and B, have masses 0.6 kg and 0.2 kg, respectively. A and B are simultaneously projected towards each other in the same straight line on a horizontal surface at speeds of 5 m s^{-1} and 2 m s^{-1}, respectively. Before A and B collide the only horizontal force acting is friction, and each particle decelerates at 0.5 m s^{-2}. The particles collide and coalesce 3 s after projection.

    a) Find the speed of each particle immediately before the collision.

    b) Find the speed of the combined particle immediately after the collision.

20. *AB* is a line of greatest slope, of length 6 m, on a smooth plane inclined at 30° to the horizontal. Particles *P* and *Q*, of masses 0.2 kg and 0.5 kg, respectively, move along *AB*, with *P* below *Q*. The particles are moving upwards, *P* at a speed of 8 m s^{-1} and *Q* at a speed of 2 m s^{-1}, when they collide at a point 3 m from *B*. Particle *P* is instantaneously at rest after the collision.

a) Determine whether *Q* reaches *B* in the subsequent motion.

b) Find the time between the collision and *P*'s arrival at *A*.

Chapter summary

Momentum

- Momentum = mass × velocity
- It is a vector quantity.
- Its units are N s.

Conservation of linear momentum

- If no external forces apply during a collision the total momentum before the collision is equal to the total momentum after the collision.

$$m_A u_A + m_B u_B = m_A v_A + m_B v_B$$

Maths in real-life

Aerodynamics

The study of aerodynamics is very important in the design of vehicles such as bikes, aeroplanes and motor vehicles as well as in the design of many other structures.

Aerodynamics is the field of science and engineering that deals with the effects of air moving around objects. Aerodynamicists use physical laws, mathematical analysis, wind tunnels and computer simulations to predict what will happen in a given situation.

Wind tunnels are used to test how planes, bikes, cars and many other objects move through the air at different speeds and to predict the forces generated. This helps engineers to improve the design of anything affected by wind. For bikes and cars the aim is for the object to be pushed towards the ground, with no lift. For aeroplanes the aim is to generate lift so that the plane can fly.

Wind tunnels can be all different shapes and sizes. They can be whole buildings, using powerful fans to test life-size objects, or small tunnels used to test small models.

▲   The huge fan in a large-scale wind tunnel

Engineers can also use computers to solve problems in aerodynamics. The computer solves complex mathematical equations that are based on Newton's laws of motion.

Aerodynamic testing is very important for cyclists. It is hard for a human being to improve their power output by 5%. This would require a lot of dedication and training. However, improving their aerodynamics can make a 10–20% difference. Aero bars instead of an upright position is the most effective change, but an Aero helmet, skin suits and shoe covers all cut down on the drag a cyclist experiences. This means that less power is required to maintain the same speed.

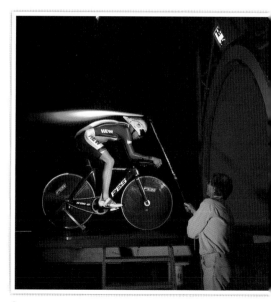

▲   Showing the effect of an Aero helmet

Daniel Bernoulli, a Swiss scientist, developed a mathematical relationship between pressure and fluid flow in the 18th century. He was a leader in fluid mechanics, the study of liquids and gasses. The Bernoulli principle is a mathematical explanation of why things can fly.

Engineers normally design wings, or airfoils, that are rounded on the top and flat on the bottom. This means that the pressure on the top of the wing is less than the pressure on the bottom of the wing, creating lift. Lift is a force that works upwards, opposing gravity.

The Wright brothers used wind tunnel testing to develop their first aircraft. The technology involved has developed significantly since then, and conducting a successful test is far more complicated than it may appear.

After a test is conducted, aerodynamicists need to make adjustments to the results in order to apply them to a full-scale aircraft and to suit the flight conditions. Judgement is very important at this stage. Any mistakes can have very serious consequences.

These adjustments can be made using theoretical and computational methods, or they can be made based on previous experiments and results.

▲ Red smoke is being used in the experiment photographed here to understand the turbulence created by an aircraft.

▼ The Wright Flyer, the first powered aircraft, flew for 12 seconds at Kitty Hawk, North Carolina on December 17, 1903.

Exam-style paper 4A

50 marks

1. A toy car of mass 200 g is moving along a straight smooth horizontal track at a speed of 3.3 m s⁻¹. The car collides with a stationary toy lorry of mass 400 g. After the collision the car and lorry move together.

   a) Find the speed of the car and lorry immediately after the collision. [3]

   b) Show that the loss in kinetic energy due to the collision is 0.726 J. [3]

2. 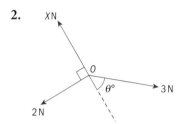 Three coplanar forces of magnitude X N, 3 N and 2 N are in equilibrium acting at a point O in the directions shown in the diagram. Evaluate θ and X. [4]

3.

   A shower curtain rail ring of mass 950 g is threaded on a rough curtain rail, which is fixed horizontally. The ring is held in equilibrium by a force of 2.8 N pulling upwards at 35° to the horizontal. Find

   i) the normal component of the contact force acting on the rail ring

   ii) the coefficient of friction between the ring and the rail if the ring is about to slip. [5]

4. A tram moves along a straight road between stops A and B. The tram is at rest when it starts at stop A and again when it reaches stop B. The tram moves at constant acceleration for the first 40 s, at a constant speed of 8 m s⁻¹ for the next 560 s and then finally at a constant deceleration of 0.08 m s⁻².

   i) Calculate the acceleration of the tram during the first 40 s. [1]

   ii) Determine the time taken for the tram to decelerate before it reaches stop B. [1]

   iii) Sketch the velocity–time graph for the journey and calculate the distance from A to B. [4]

   iv) Two people along the road record the tram's speed as 6 m s⁻¹, one while it is accelerating and the other while it is decelerating. Calculate the distance between these two people. [3]

5.

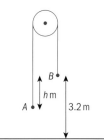

Particle A of mass $0.3\,\text{kg}$ and particle B of mass $0.5\,\text{kg}$ are attached at either end of a light inextensible string that passes over a smooth pulley. A is hanging $h\,\text{m}$ below B, which is being held at rest $3.2\,\text{m}$ above the floor. Both parts of the string are vertical. B is released and both particles begin to move. When B reaches the floor it remains at rest while A continues to move vertically upwards. A reaches its maximum height when it is $6.2\,\text{m}$ above the floor. Ignoring air resistance, calculate the velocity of the particles immediately before B reaches the floor and hence evaluate h. [6]

6. A racing car is designed to accelerate rapidly along a straight track. The car starts from rest at a point O and accelerates until it crosses the finishing line at a speed of $85\,\text{m}\,\text{s}^{-1}$. While the car is moving along the track t seconds after leaving O its acceleration is $(6 + 0.4t)\,\text{m}\,\text{s}^{-2}$. Calculate

  i) the time taken by the car to reach the finishing line [4]

  ii) the distance travelled by the car along the track from O to the finishing line. [3]

7. A ball A is thrown vertically upwards at a speed of $16\,\text{m}\,\text{s}^{-1}$ from a point P. One second after the projection of A a second ball B is also thrown vertically upwards from P at a speed of $16\,\text{m}\,\text{s}^{-1}$. Ignoring air resistance, find

  i) the time that A has been moving when the balls collide [5]

  ii) the height above P at which the balls collide. [2]

8. A force F is acting vertically upwards on a body of mass $10\,\text{kg}$. The body moves vertically from rest to a point A that is at a height of $5\,\text{m}$ above its starting point. The body has a speed of $7\,\text{m}\,\text{s}^{-1}$ at A.

  i) Find the work done by F. [4]

It is now given that F is constant.

  ii) Find F. [2]

1. Two particles A and B have masses m kg and 3 kg, respectively. The particles are moving towards each other along a straight horizontal line. The speeds of A and B immediately before they collide are $2\,\text{m s}^{-1}$ and $3\,\text{m s}^{-1}$, respectively.

   Given that the particles move in opposite directions after the collision, each at a speed of $0.5\,\text{m s}^{-1}$, find the value of m. [3]

2.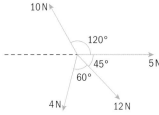

   Four coplanar forces act at a point. The magnitude of the forces are 10 N, 5 N, 12 N and 4 N, and the directions in which the forces act are shown in the diagram. Calculate the magnitude and direction of the resultant of the four forces. [5]

3. A particle M of mass 350 g rests on a rough plane inclined at an angle θ to the horizontal, where $\cos\theta = 0.96$. A force is acting on M. Its magnitude is 0.45 N, and it acts at an angle θ above the line of greatest slope of the plane. It is just sufficient to prevent the particle from sliding down the plane. Determine

   i) the normal component of the contact force on M [2]

   ii) the frictional component of the contact force on M [3]

   iii) the coefficient of friction between M and the plane. [2]

4. A car travels along a straight road from A to B, a distance of 5 km in 655 s.
   The car starts from rest at A and accelerates uniformly for T_1 s at $0.4\,\text{m s}^{-1}$. It reaches a speed $V\,\text{m s}^{-1}$ and then travels at constant speed for T_2 s. It then decelerates uniformly for 40 s before coming to rest at B.

   i) Sketch the velocity–time graph for the motion of the car. [1]

   ii) Express T_1 and the final deceleration d in terms of V. [2]

   iii) Express the total distance travelled in terms of V and show that
   $V^2 - 508V + 4000 = 0$. Hence find the value of V. [4]

5. 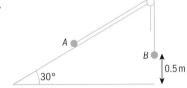 Particles A of mass 0.6 kg and B of mass 0.9 kg are connected by a light inextensible string that passes over a smooth pulley that is fixed at the top of a smooth sloping flat surface that is inclined at an angle of 30° to the horizontal. Particle A lies on the slope and particle B is released from rest and falls 0.5 m to the floor, where it remains at rest. Particle A then continues to move up the slope.

   i)   Show that the acceleration of the particles is $4\,\mathrm{m\,s^{-2}}$ before B hits the floor and find the tension in the string.   [4]

   ii) Calculate the speed of the particles just before particle B reaches the floor.   [2]

   iii) Assuming that it does not reach the pulley, calculate the further distance that particle A travels up the slope.   [4]

6. The resistance to the motion of a lorry of mass 5 tonnes is kv, where $v\,\mathrm{m\,s^{-1}}$ is the lorry's speed. With the engine working at 66 kW the lorry can attain a greatest steady speed of $12\,\mathrm{m\,s^{-1}}$ up a straight road that is inclined at $\sin^{-1}\dfrac{1}{20}$ to the horizontal.

   i)   Show that $k = 250$.   [4]

   ii) Determine the greatest steady speed that the lorry can go down this slope with the engine still working at 66 kW.   [4]

7. A block of mass 25 kg is dragged 30 m up a slope inclined at 5° to the horizontal by a rope inclined at 20° to the slope. The tension in the rope is 100 N and the resistance to the motion of the block is 70 N. The block is initially at rest. Calculate

   i)   the work done by the tension in the rope   [2]

   ii) the change in the potential energy of the block   [2]

   iii) the speed of the block after it has moved 30 m up the slope.   [4]

Answers

The answers given here are concise. However, when answering exam-style questions, you should show as many steps in your working as possible. Where not exact, answers are given correct to three (3) significant figures.

1 Straight-line motion and graphs

Skills check page 2

1. 1200
2. **a)** 0.375 **b)** −0.5
3. **a)** 6 s **b)** 40 s **c)** 0.2 s
4. **a)** 144 m **b)** 4 m **c)** 15 m
5. **a)** 3 m s⁻¹ **b)** 1.5 m s⁻¹ **c)** 0.2 m s⁻¹
6. **a)** 100 m s⁻¹ **b)** 6 m s⁻¹
7. **a)** 3 m s⁻² **b)** −2 m s⁻²
8. 3 s

Exercise 1.1 page 5

1. **a)**
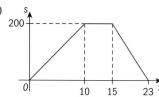
   b) −4 m s⁻¹
2. **a)**
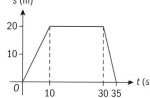
   b) −25 m s⁻¹
3. **a)**
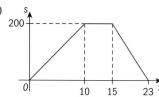
   b) 11 m
4. **a)** 1.5 m s⁻¹ **b)** 0 **c)** −0.5 m s⁻¹
5. **a)** 1.6 m s⁻¹ **b)** 0 **c)** 0.8 m s⁻¹

6. **a)** −1.125 m s⁻¹
   b) 0 **c)** −0.75 m s⁻¹
7. **a)** 320 m **b)** −16 m s⁻¹
8. **a)** 0.667 **b)** 2 s
9. **a)** −8 m s⁻¹ **b)** 72
10. **a)** 1.6 **b)** −8 m **c)** 12 m
    d) −20 m **e)** −2 m s⁻¹

Exercise 1.2 page 12

1.

2.
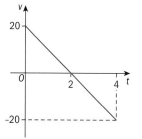
3.
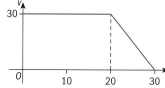
4. **a)** 0.167 m s⁻² and −0.1 m s⁻²
   b) 450 m **c)** 3.46 m s⁻¹
5. **a)** 1.6 m s⁻², 1.6 m s⁻²
   b) 240 m **c)** 660 m
6. **a)** 15 m s⁻¹ **b)** 0.75 m s⁻² **c)** 375 m
7. **a)** 30 s **b)** 750 m **c)** 4.17 m s⁻¹
8. **a)** 2.5 m s⁻², 0 m s⁻², −2.5 m s⁻², 0 m s⁻²,
   −2.5 m s⁻², 0 m s⁻², 2.5 m s⁻²
   b) 25 m **c)** 35 m
   d) 18th floor, 4th floor
9. **a)** 24 m s⁻¹ **b)** 3.43 m s⁻²
   c) −3 m s⁻² **d)** 1.75 s and 23 s
10. **a)** 10 m s⁻¹
    b) −2 m s⁻² and −0.625 m s⁻²
    c) 10.6 m s⁻¹

11. **a)** 5 m s⁻¹ or 1 m s⁻¹ **b)** 2 s or 2.8 s
12. **a)** 4 m s⁻¹ **b)** 4 s
13. **a)** 45 m **b)** 5 s **c)** −30 m s⁻¹
    d) 15 m s⁻¹ **e)** 11.25 m **f)** 8 s

Summary exercise 1 page 16

1. **a)** 0.4 m
   b)
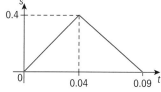
2. **a)**
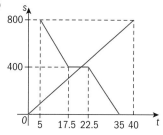
   b) 433 m, 21.7 s
   c) the train moving from B to A (39 s)
3. **a)** 120 m **b)** 6.67 m s⁻¹
   c) 15 m s⁻² **d)** 90 m
4. **a)** 9.83 s **b)** 3.6 m s⁻²
5. **a)**
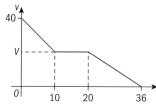
   b) 20 m s⁻¹ **c)** 18.3 m s⁻¹
6. **a)**
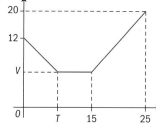
   b) 2 **c)** 7.8

2 Constant-acceleration formulae

Skills check page 18

1. **a)** 14   **b)** 18   **c)** 2
2. **a)** $u = 4$ **b)** $a = \frac{8}{3} = 2\frac{2}{3}$ **c)** $t = 1\frac{1}{2}$
3. **a)** 2, 6   **b)** -0.281 or 1.78
   c) 0.869 or -1.54

Exercise 2.1 page 23

1. 128 m
2. 40 m
3. $15\,\text{m s}^{-1}$
4. $5\,\text{m s}^{-1}$
5. $9.8\,\text{m s}^{-2}$
6. 20 s
7. 2 s
8. 12 m
9. $4\,\text{m s}^{-1}$
10. $23\,\text{m s}^{-1}$
11. **a)** 500 m   **b)** $20\,\text{m s}^{-1}$
12. **a)** 31 m   **b)** 5 s
13. 37 m
14. 17.1 m
15. **a)** $4.25\ \text{m s}^{-1}$ **b)** $2.75\ \text{m s}^{-1}$

Exercise 2.2 page 26

1. $6\,\text{m s}^{-1}$
2. 3.10 s
3. 16.2 m
4. $5\,\text{m s}^{-1}$, 30 m
5. 31.25 m, 5 s
6. **a)** $15.6\,\text{m s}^{-1}$ **b)** 2.76 s
7. **a)** 2.45 s   **b)** $24.5\,\text{m s}^{-1}$
8. **a)** 0.8 s   **b)** 4.2 m   **c)** $9.17\,\text{m s}^{-1}$
9. 54 m
10. **a) i)** 1 s   **ii)** 5 s   **b)** 4 s
11. **a)** $20\,\text{m s}^{-1}$ **b)** 20 m   **c)** 2.83 s
12. **a)** $5.74\,\text{m s}^{-1}$ **b)** 4.05 m   **c)** 1.36 s
13. **a)** Proof   **b)** $6\,\text{m s}^{-1}$
    c) $1\,\text{m s}^{-1}$ upwards, $1\,\text{m s}^{-1}$ downwards

Summary exercise 2 page 27

1. **a)** 2 s   **b)** 2 s
2. **a)** $320\,\text{m s}^{-1}$ **b)** 1600 m
3. **a)** 11 m   **b)** 10.1 s

4. $7.22\,\text{s}$, $47.2\,\text{m s}^{-1}$
5. 0.917 s
6. 25.8 s, 200 m
7. 68.3 s, $46.8\,\text{m s}^{-1}$
8. **a)** $9.6\,\text{m s}^{-1}$ **b)** 13.5 s
9. **a)** $0.2, 0.92$ **b)** 0.72 s   **c)** 1.176 m

3 Variable acceleration

Skills check page 29

1. **a)** $2x - 2$ **b)** $-\dfrac{1}{x^2} + \dfrac{2}{x^3}$
   c) $\dfrac{1}{2\sqrt{x}}$
2. Minimum: $(0, 0)$; maximum: $(1.5, 6.75)$
3. **a)** $x^3 + 2x^2 + c$ **b)** $-\dfrac{1}{2x} + c$
   c) $\dfrac{2}{3}x^{\frac{3}{2}} + c$ **d)** $\dfrac{1}{8}(1 + 2x)^4 + c$
   e) $\dfrac{1}{3}(2x - 1)^{\frac{3}{2}} + c$
4. $\dfrac{2x^3}{3} - \dfrac{x^2}{2} - x + c, -\dfrac{1}{6}$
5. 17

Exercise 3.1 page 32

1. $t = 1$
2. $v = 6\dfrac{1}{3}$
3. $a = 3t^2 - 12t + 9, v = 4$
4. $v = 6t^2 + 2t - 1, a = 12t + 2$
5. $v = 8t^3 - 27, a = 24t^2, a = 54$
6. $v = 6t^2 - 6t, a = 12t - 6$,
   $s = -73$ and $s = -72$
7. $a = 2t - \dfrac{1}{4t^2}, t = \dfrac{1}{2}, v = \dfrac{5}{4}$
8. **a)** $t = 9\,\text{s}$ **b)** $t = 4\,\text{s}, a = -\dfrac{3}{32}\,\text{m s}^{-2}$
9. **a)** $t = 1$ hour   **b)** $s = 20\,\text{km}$
   c) $v = 35.6\,\text{km h}^{-1}$
10. **a)** $v = 6t^2 - 18t + 12$
    b) $t = 1$ and 2
    c) $s = 1$ and 0 **d)** $s = 11$

Exercise 3.2 page 36

1. Proof
2. $s = 3t^5 - 4t^3 - 30; s = -31\,\text{m}$
3. $v = 12t - t^3 - 8, s = 6t^2 - \dfrac{1}{4}t^4 - 8t - 2$
4. $s = 28$
5. $s = \dfrac{11}{2}$
6. $v = t^2 - \dfrac{1}{3}t^3 + 3, v = 4\dfrac{1}{3}, s = 7\dfrac{1}{3}$

7. $s = \dfrac{(1 + 2t)^4 + 3}{2}$
8. $v = 5(2t - 1)^{\frac{3}{2}}, s = (2t - 1)^{\frac{5}{2}}$
9. $s = t^2 + \dfrac{2}{t}, a = 2 + \dfrac{4}{t^3}$
10. $v = 1\dfrac{1}{8}, x = 1\dfrac{1}{8}$

Summary exercise 3 page 38

1. **a)** $2.18\,\text{m s}^{-1}$ **b)** 25 m
2. **a)** 233 m   **b)** 24 s
   c) $19.1\,\text{m s}^{-1}$
3. **a)** $5\,\text{m s}^{-1}$ **b)** 7.25 s
   c) 10.5 m
4. **a)** $t = 30$
   b) 6400 m
5. $t = 5\,\text{s}, x = 4.5\,\text{m}, v = -2\,\text{m s}^{-1}$ and 0

4 Forces and resultants

Skills check page 42

1. 53.1°
2. $a = 3.84\,\text{cm}$
3. $\theta = 101.5°$

Exercise 4.1 page 44

1. **a)** 21.7 N, 10.9°   **b)** 20.3 N, 24.7°
   c) 13.5 N, 59.3°
2. **a)** 493 N, 12.3°   **b)** 250 N, 36.9°
   c) 851 N, 20.4°   **d)** 164 N, 53.1°
3. 363 N, 8.7° below horizontal
4. 95.5°, 45.3°
5. 66.6 N
6. 47.1°

Exercise 4.2 page 47

1. **a)** 14.1 N   **b)** 14.1 N
2. **a)** $-13.0\,\text{N}$ **b)** $-7.5\,\text{N}$
3. **a)** 12.5 N   **b)** $-21.7\,\text{N}$
4. **a)** $-7.85\,\text{N}$ **b)** 3.66 N
5. **a)** $-24.5\,\text{N}$ **b)** $-24.5\,\text{N}$

Exercise 4.3 page 51

1. **a)** $X = 38.3\,\text{N}, Y = 32.1\,\text{N}$
   b) $\theta = 138.6°, X = 10.6\,\text{N}$
   c) $X = 0.695\,\text{N}, Y = 3.94\,\text{N}$
   d) $X = 20\,\text{N}, Y = 32.3\,\text{N}$
   e) $\theta = 68.3°, X = 8.07\,\text{N}$

f) $\theta = 146.5°$, $X = 6.87\,\text{N}$

g) $T = 3.34\,\text{N}$, $\theta = 125.0°$

2. a) $P = 5.57\,\text{N}$, $Q = 4.47\,\text{N}$

b) $P = 9.20\,\text{N}$, $Q = 7.96\,\text{N}$

c) $P = 46.5\,\text{N}$, $Q = 13.5\,\text{N}$

3. Both $56.6\,\text{N}$

4. $T = 17.3\,\text{N}$, $F = 8.66\,\text{N}$

5. $F = 13.2\,\text{N}$, $T = 22.2\,\text{N}$

6. $T = 44.9\,\text{N}$, $F = 59.6\,\text{N}$

Summary exercise 4 page 52

1. i) a) $-5.82\,\text{N}$ **b)** $7.43\,\text{N}$

c) $9.44\,\text{N}$

ii) a) $x = 14.5\,\text{N}$ **b)** $y = 8.49\,\text{N}$

c) $16.8\,\text{N}$

iii) a) $x = 2.66\,\text{N}$ **b)** $y = 5.66\,\text{N}$

c) $6.25\,\text{N}$

iv) a) $x = 2\,\text{N}$ **b)** $y = 3.46\,\text{N}$

c) $4\,\text{N}$

v) a) $x = 3.10\,\text{N}$ **b)** $y = 1.64\,\text{N}$

c) $3.50\,\text{N}$

vi) a) $x = -6.02\,\text{N}$ **b)** $y = -3.64\,\text{N}$;

c) $7.04\,\text{N}$

vii) a) $x = 4.94\,\text{N}$;   **b)** $y = 2.98\,\text{N}$

c) $5.76\,\text{N}$

2. a) $x = 3.40\,\text{N}$

b) $y = 11.9\,\text{N}$; $R = 12.4\,\text{N}$

b) $x = -5.66\,\text{N}$; $y = 2.19\,\text{N}$; $R = 6.07\,\text{N}$

c) $x = -4.93\,\text{N}$; $y = 3.63\,\text{N}$; $R = 6.12\,\text{N}$

d) $x = -2 + 3\sqrt{3}\,\text{N}$; $y = 5\,\text{N}$; $R = 5.93\,\text{N}$

3. a) $R = 4.91\,\text{N}$, $\theta = 6.85°$

b) $R = 4.26\,\text{N}$, $\theta = 35.1°$

c) $R = 7.46\,\text{N}$, $\theta = 27.3°$ above the negative x-axis

d) $R = 10.43\,\text{N}$, $\theta = 25.5°$ below the negative x-axis

4. a) $X = 74.3\,\text{N}$ **b)** $X = 40\,\text{N}$;

c) $X = 12.2\,\text{N}$ **d)** $X = 19.2\,\text{N}$

e) $X = 22.5\,\text{N}$ **f)** $X = 25.2\,\text{N}$

5. a) $A = 2.88\,\text{N}$; $B = 11.6\,\text{N}$

b) $A = -5.73\,\text{N}$; $B = 28.4\,\text{N}$

c) $A = 14.1\,\text{N}$; $B = 1.79\,\text{N}$

d) $A = 37.9\,\text{N}$; $B = 41.8\,\text{N}$

6. $R = 573\,\text{N}$ at $14.5°$ to the $350\,\text{N}$ force

7. $R = 73.1\,\text{N}$ at $50.0°$ to the $47\,\text{N}$ force

8. $X = 173\,\text{N}$

9. $3\,\text{N}$

10. $40°$

11. $5.48\,\text{N}$

12. Proof

13. Proof

14. $R = 53.3\,\text{N}$, $\theta = 19.0°$ to the $20\,\text{N}$ force

15. $3.98\,\text{N}$, $52.9°$ to $5\,\text{N}$ force

16. $85.9°$, $8.5\,\text{N}$

17. $16.2\,\text{N}$, $8.9°$

5 Newton's laws

Skills check page 57

1. a) $s = 24$ **b)** $u = 12$ **c)** $s = 2.5$

2. horizontal $= 10.4\,\text{N}$, vertical $= 6\,\text{N}$

Exercise 5.1 page 61

1. a) Slides backwards.

b) Stays where it is.

c) Slides forwards.

2. $a = 3\,\text{m s}^{-2}$

3. $m = 15\,\text{kg}$

4. $F = 48\,\text{N}$

5. $t = 4\,\text{s}$

6. $v = 12\,\text{m s}^{-1}$

7. $F = -0.2\,\text{N}$

8. $F = 156\,\text{N}$

9. $s = 2.81\,\text{m}$

10. a) $T = 20\,500\,\text{N}$ **b)** $T = 6980\,\text{N}$

c) $m = 770\,\text{kg}$

Exercise 5.2 page 63

1. i) $1310\,\text{N}$ **ii)** $14\,900\,\text{N}$

2. $11.8°$

3. Parallel: $14\,100\,\text{N}$, perpendicular: $16\,900\,\text{N}$;

a) Parallel: $12\,700\,\text{N}$, perpendicular: $15\,200\,\text{N}$

Parallel: $11\,500\,\text{N}$, perpendicular: $13\,700\,\text{N}$

Parallel: $10\,500\,\text{N}$, perpendicular: $12\,600\,\text{N}$

b) $4290\,\text{N}$

4. $90.1\,\text{N}$

Exercise 5.3 page 65

1. a) $P = 30\,\text{N}$, $Q = 60\,\text{N}$

b) $P = 24\,\text{N}$, $Q = 18\,\text{N}$

2.

3. $23.4\,\text{N}$

4. $T = 4 + 1.5g$

5. $\theta = 8.7°$, $a = 0.0925\,\text{m s}^{-2}$

6. $a = 2.65\,\text{m s}^{-2}$, $s = 47.7\,\text{m}$

7. $L = 932\,\text{N}$, $R = 98.0\,\text{N}$

Exercise 5.4 page 68

1. $a = 0.5\,\text{m s}^{-2}$, $T = 3.5\,\text{N}$

2. a) $a = 2\,\text{m s}^{-2}$, $T = 5\,\text{N}$

b) $t = 10\,\text{s}$

3. $a = 2\,\text{m s}^{-2}$, $T = 24\,\text{N}$, resultant force $= 48\,\text{N}$

4. a) $a = 6\,\text{m s}^{-2}$, $T = 32\,\text{N}$

b) $t = 3\,\text{s}$

5. a) $a = \dfrac{10}{3}\,\text{m s}^{-2}$

b) $v = 10\,\text{m s}^{-1}$

6. $\dfrac{2}{3}g$

7. $\dfrac{g}{12}$; $\dfrac{11}{6}g$

8. $0.904\,\text{m s}^{-2}$

9. a) $a - 0.375\,\text{m s}^{-2}$

b) $T = 6100\,\text{N}$

10. $F = 40\,200\,\text{N}$

Summary exercise 5 page 70

1. $T = 205\,\text{N}$, $R = 385\,\text{N}$, $\theta = 20°$

2. a) i) $676\,\text{N}$ **ii)** $8480\,\text{N}$

b) i) $611\,\text{N}$ **ii)** $7660\,\text{N}$

3. $a = 3\,\text{m s}^{-2}$, $T = 21$

4. a) $a = 0.4\,\text{m s}^{-2}$ **b)** $s = 203\,\text{m}$

5. a) $a = 0.46\,\text{m s}^{-2}$, $T = 2160\,\text{N}$

b) $t = 14.4\,\text{s}$, $T = -40\,\text{N}$

The force in the tow-bar is no longer a tension force, but a thrust.

6. a) $F = 132\,\text{N}$

b) $s = 120\,\text{m}$

6 Friction

Skills check page 73

1. **a)** $\cos A = \dfrac{15}{17}$; angle $CAB = 28.1°$

   b) $\cos Q = \dfrac{3}{5}$; angle $PQR = 53.1°$

   c) Longest side $XZ = 25\,\text{cm}$; angle $ZXY = 53.1°$

2. **a)** $a = \dfrac{v - u}{t}$

   b) $a = \dfrac{2(s - ut)}{t^2}$

   c) $t = \dfrac{g^3}{p^4}$

3. **a)** $v = \pm 6.24$

   b) $s = 46.5$

   c) $p = \pm 0.622$

Exercise 6.1 page 77

1. No motion will occur.
2. No motion will occur.
3. Motion will occur.
4. Motion will occur.
5. No motion will occur.
6. Motion will occur.

Exercise 6.2 page 80

1. **a)** Motion down the plane; $F_{max} = 28.7\,\text{N}$

   b) Motion down the plane; $F_{max} = 32.5\,\text{N}$

   c) Motion up the plane; $F_{max} = 15.8\,\text{N}$

2. Force required to maintain limiting equilibrium is $1207\,\text{N}$.

3. $123\,\text{N}$
4. 0.929
5. 0.320
6. 0.318

Summary exercise 6 page 82

1. $4.51\,\text{m s}^{-2}$
2. 0.774
3. $-1.66\,\text{m s}^{-2}$, $4.81\,\text{m}$
4. **a)** $F_{max} > 20\,\text{N}$, no motion

   b) $F_{max} > 11\sqrt{3}\,\text{N}$, no motion

   c) $F_{max} < 36\sqrt{6}\,\text{N}$, motion with $a = 10.8\,\text{m s}^{-2}$

5. **a)** Since $260\,\text{N} < 306\,\text{N}$, no motion takes place.

   b) Since $200\,\text{N} < 376\,\text{N}$, no motion takes place.

   c) Since $900\,\text{N} > 630\,\text{N}$, motion will take place.

   d) Since $283\,\text{N} > 173\,\text{N}$, motion will take place.

6. $\mu = 0.700$
7. $\mu = 0.190$
8. $\mu = 0.742$
9. **a)** $\theta = 12.3°$

   b) $\mu_{min} = 0.218$

10. $\mu = 0.386$
11. $s = 1.44\,\text{m s}^{-2}$
12. $\mu = 0.268$
13. $a = 0.333\,\text{m s}^{-2}$

7 Work and energy

Skills check page 86

1. **a)** $25\,\text{N}$ **b)** $91.9\,\text{N}$

   c) $51.4\,\text{N}$

2. **a)** $730\,\text{N}$ **b)** $4590\,\text{N}$

Exercise 7.1 page 89

1. $800\,\text{J}$
2. $12\,800\,\text{J}$
3. $2700\,\text{J}$
4. $1260\,\text{J}$
5. $3900\,\text{J}$
6. $130\,\text{J}$
7. $7.71\,\text{J}$
8. $8\,\text{N}$
9. $20.3\,\text{N}$
10. **a)** $550\,\text{m}$, $66\,000\,\text{J}$

    b) $607\,\text{m}$, $68\,500\,\text{J}$

Exercise 7.2 page 90

1. **a)** $40\,\text{J}$ **b)** $9\,\text{J}$

   c) $60\,000\,\text{J}$ **d)** $20\,\text{J}$

2. **a)** $7700\,\text{J}$ **b)** $125\,\text{J}$

3. **a)** $12.5\,\text{J}$ **b)** $43\,200\,\text{J}$

4. $5.42\,\text{m s}^{-1}$

5. **a)** $0.2\,\text{J}$ **b)** $3.58\,\text{m s}^{-1}$

6. **a)** $1500\,\text{J}$ **b)** $1.58\,\text{m s}^{-1}$

Exercise 7.4 page 93

1. **a)** $680\,\text{J}$ **b)** $187\,000\,\text{J}$

   c) $66.5\,\text{m s}^{-1}$, assuming no air resistance

2. **a)** $7.2\,\text{m}$ **b)** $18.7\,\text{m}$ **c)** $12\,\text{m s}^{-1}$

3. **a)** $700\,\text{kJ}$ **b)** $699\,\text{kJ}$

4. $17.3\,\text{m s}^{-1}$

5. $3.2\,\text{m}$

6. **a)** $25.6\,\text{J}$ **b)** $12.8\,\text{m}$ **c)** $1.5\,\text{m}$

7. $11.1\,\text{m s}^{-1}$

8. $7.2\,\text{m}$

9. $3\,\text{m}$

10. **a)** $12.0\,\text{m s}^{-1}$ **b)** $12.0\,\text{m s}^{-1}$
    c) $15\,\text{m s}^{-1}$ **d)** $11.3\,\text{m}$

11. $5.33\,\text{m}$

12. $44.1\,\text{m}$

Exercise 7.5 page 98

1. $4.5\,\text{N}$
2. $80\,500\,\text{J}$, $1610\,\text{N}$
3. $588\,880\,\text{J}$
4. $1875\,\text{N}$
5. $175\,600\,\text{N}$
6. **a)** $2570\,\text{J}$ **b)** $9.26\,\text{m s}^{-1}$
7. $5.37\,\text{m s}^{-1}$
8. **a)** $9.49\,\text{m s}^{-1}$ **b)** $910\,\text{J}$, $75.8\,\text{N}$
9. **a)** $60\,\text{J}$ **b)** $5.39\,\text{m s}^{-1}$
10. $10.1\,\text{m s}^{-1}$
11. **a)** $6\,\text{m s}^{-2}$ **b)** Proof

Summary exercise 7 page 100

1. **a)** $5.66\,\text{m s}^{-1}$ **b)** $40\,\text{m}$
2. $13.5\,\text{m s}^{-1}$
3. **a)** $902\,\text{J}$ **b)** $6.73\,\text{m s}^{-1}$
4. **a)** **i)** $45\,\text{J}$ **ii)** $5000\,\text{J}$
   b) $32.8°$
5. $7.07\,\text{m s}^{-1}$
6. $5.95\,\text{m s}^{-1}$
7. $3700\,\text{N}$
8. $8270\,\text{J}$
9. $97.9\,\text{N}$
10. $114\,\text{m}$
11. **a)** $2.93\,\text{N}$ **b)** $7.85\,\text{N}$
    c) $v = 6.57\,\text{m s}^{-1}$

8 Power

Skills check page 102

1. **a)** $0.8\,\text{m s}^{-2}$ **b)** $1.07\,\text{m s}^{-2}$

2. **a)** $6000\,\text{J}$ **b)** $480\,\text{kJ}$ **c)** $500\,\text{N}$

Exercise 8.1 page 105

1. 1800 W
2. 1600 W
3. 180 W
4. 21 W
5. **a)** $6.67\,\text{m s}^{-1}$ **b)** $11.3\,\text{m s}^{-1}$
   c) $15.3\,\text{m s}^{-1}$
6. 778 N
7. 540 W
8. 625
9. **a)** $10.4\,\text{m s}^{-1}$ **b)** $4.51\,\text{m s}^{-1}$
   c) $15.5\,\text{m s}^{-1}$
10. 6370 N
11. **a)** 6250 kW **b)** $13.9\,\text{m s}^{-1}$
12. **a)** 70 900 W **b)** 98.7 m
    c) 11.0 s

Exercise 8.2 page 108

1. $0.214\,\text{m s}^{-2}$
2. **a)** $4.69\,\text{m s}^{-2}$
   b) $0.938\,\text{m s}^{-2}$ **c)** $48\,\text{m s}^{-1}$
3. **a)** $1.7\,\text{m s}^{-2}$ **b)** $3.48\,\text{m s}^{-1}$
   c) $26.7\,\text{m s}^{-1}$
4. **a)** 1800 N **b)** $0.0225\,\text{m s}^{-2}$
5. **a)** 11 200 W **b)** $0.0794\,\text{m s}^{-2}$
6. **a)** 1250 N **b)** 2.17
   c) 61 300 W
7. **a)** Proof **b)** $12.5\,\text{m s}^{-1}$
8. **a)** $1.4°$ **b)** $5\,\text{m s}^{-1}$
9. 16 000, 1500
10. **a)** 31.25 **b)** $28.4\,\text{m s}^{-1}$
    c) $56.3\,\text{m s}^{-1}$

Summary exercise 8 page 110

1. 200 W
2. 300 W
3. **a)** 16 **b)** 320 N **c)** 6400 W
4. **a)** 500 N **b)** $22.4\,\text{m s}^{-1}$
5. **a)** $50\,\text{m s}^{-1}$ **b)** $2\,\text{m s}^{-2}$
6. 165 000, 3660
7. **a)** 17.28 **b)** 2220 kg **c)** 22.1
8. **a)** Proof **b)** $10P = 9k - 90, 30, 18$
   c) $24.5\,\text{m s}^{-1}$
9. 19 600 W
10. 1000 N

9 Momentum

Skills check page 112

1. **a)** $v = 4$ **b)** $v = 1.5$ **c)** $m = 3$
2. **a) i)** 22.5 J **ii)** 60 000 J
   b) 6.3 J

Exercise 9.1 page 114

1. **a)** 24 000 N s **b)** 2.4 N s
   c) 120 N s **d)** 11 040 000 N s
   e) 42 000 N s
2. 0.32 N s
3. 0.224 N s
4. 42 000 N s
5. 6.88 N s
6. 3.48 N s (3 s.f.)

Exercise 9.2 page 117

1. **a)** $2.5\,\text{m s}^{-1}$ **b)** $10\,\text{m s}^{-1}$
   c) $3.0\,\text{m s}^{-1}$ **d)** $1.33\,\text{m s}^{-1}$
2. $1.4\,\text{m s}^{-1}$, in the reverse direction
3. Proof
4. $8.82\,\text{m s}^{-1}$ (3 s.f.)
5. 12
6. **a)** $3.86\,\text{m s}^{-1}$ (3 s.f.)
   b) $0.429\,\text{m s}^{-1}$ (3 s.f.)
7. $18\,\text{m s}^{-1}$
8. **a)** $4\,\text{m s}^{-1}$ **b)** 2 N s
9. **a)** $1.48\,\text{m s}^{-1}$ **b)** 0.216
10. **a)** $0.5\,\text{m s}^{-1}$; direction reverses
    b) 1.5 J

Summary exercise 9 page 120

1. **a)** 1.74 N s
   b) $0.975\,\text{m s}^{-1}$; direction reverses
2. $0.5\,\text{m s}^{-1}$, in the direction of the 80 g
   mass before the collision
3. 2250
4. **a)** $200.4\,\text{m s}^{-1}$ **b)** 64 000 J
5. 0.429 (3 s.f.)
6. **a)** $0.727\,\text{m s}^{-1}$ (3 s.f.); B changes
   direction.
   b) i) $8\,\text{m s}^{-1}$ **ii)** 18 000 N s
7. $2\,\text{m s}^{-1}$
8. **a)** 0.4 **b)** 0.28, 0.6, 0.36
9. A: $1.5\,\text{m s}^{-1}$, B: $2\,\text{m s}^{-1}$
10. **a)** $8.75\,\text{m s}^{-1}$ **b)** $3.5\,\text{m s}^{-1}$
11. $3.5\,\text{m s}^{-1}$

12. 100
13. **a)** $4\,\text{m s}^{-1}$ **b)** 12
14. **a)** $1\,\text{m s}^{-1}$ **b)** $-1.8\,\text{N s}$ **c)** 1.8 J
15. **a)** 1200 **b)** 3600 N s
16. **a)** $1.6\,\text{m s}^{-1}$ **b)** 0.933 or 2.8
17. **a)** Proof **b)** 1.5
18. **a)** $0.5\,\text{m s}^{-1}$
    b) i) 0.85 N s; proof **ii)** $0.607\,\text{m s}^{-1}$
19. **a)** A: $3.5\,\text{m s}^{-1}$; B: $0.5\,\text{m s}^{-1}$
    b) $2.5\,\text{m s}^{-1}$
20. **a)** Q does not reach B. **b)** 1.10 s

Exam-style paper 4A page 126

1. **a)** $v = 1.1\,\text{m s}^{-1}$ **b)** Proof
2. $\theta = 41.8°$
   $X = 2.24\,\text{N}$
3. **i)** $R = 7.89\,\text{N}$ **ii)** $\mu = 0.291$
4. **i)** $0.2\,\text{m s}^{-2}$ **ii)** 100 s
   iii) 5040 m **iv)** 4725 m
5. $h = 1\,\text{m}$, $4\,\text{m s}^{-1}$ up and $4\,\text{m s}^{-1}$ down
6. **i)** $t = 10.5\,\text{s}$ **ii)** $s = 408\,\text{m}$
7. **i)** 2.1 s **ii)** 11.6 m
8. **i)** 745 J **ii)** 149 N

Exam-style paper 4B page 128

1. $m = 4.2$
2. 8.31 N, 26.3° below the positive x-axis
3. **i)** $R = 3.23\,\text{N}$
   ii) $F = 0.548\,\text{N}$
   iii) 0.169
4. **i)**

   ii) $T_1 = 2.5V$, deceleration $= \dfrac{V}{40}$
   iii) $V = 8\,\text{m s}^{-1}$
5. **i)** Proof and $T = 5.4\,\text{N}$
   ii) $2\,\text{m s}^{-1}$
   iii) 0.8 m
6. **i)** Proof **ii)** $22\,\text{m s}^{-1}$
7. **i)** 2820 J **ii)** 654 J **iii)** $2.29\,\text{m s}^{-1}$

Glossary

Command words

calculate   Work out from given facts, figures and information.

describe   Give the characteristics and main features.

determine   Establish with certainty.

evaluate   Judge or calculate the quality/importance/amount/value of something.

explain   Set out purposes/reasons/mechanisms, or make the relationship between things clear, with supporting evidence.

show that   Provide structured evidence that leads to a given result.

sketch   Make a simple freehand drawing showing the key features.

state   Express in clear terms.

verify   Confirm that a given statement/result is true.

Mathematical terms

acceleration   A vector quantity that tells us the rate at which the velocity of a body is changing.

acceleration due to gravity   The acceleration of a body in free fall; the numerical value for calculations is taken to be $10 \, \text{m s}^{-2}$.

body   An object: a collection of matter with an identifiable boundary.

braking distance   The distance that a vehicle travels from the point where its brakes are applied to the point where it stops.

coefficient of friction   The ratio of the maximum frictional force to the normal reaction force.

component   The resolved part of a force.

conservative system   The total of the system's potential energy and kinetic energy is constant.

constant acceleration formulae   Formulae (sometimes known as the *suvat* equations) that relate displacement, velocity and time for motion with constant acceleration.

cosine rule   In a triangle ABC with sides of length a, b and c: $a^2 = b^2 + c^2 - 2bc \cos A$.

definite integral   An integral evaluated between two limits.

derivative   The gradient of a function at any point.

displacement   A vector quantity that gives the position of a body relative to an origin.

displacement–time graph   A graph showing the motion of a particle in one dimension with displacement on the vertical axis and time on the horizontal axis.

equilibrium   The state of a body when at rest or moving with constant velocity; the resultant of forces on the body is zero.

force   An influence that can change the motion of a body.

free fall   The motion of a body where the only force acting upon it is gravity.

friction   The force between the surfaces of two objects in contact with each other that resists their relative motion .

gradient   How steep a line is (its slope).

gravitational potential energy   The energy given to a particle that depends on its position in a gravitational field.

inclined plane   A sloping surface.

indefinite integral   An integral with no limits that needs to include a constant of integration.

integral   Anti-derivative: a function of which a given function is the derivative; often used to express the area under the curve of a graph of the given function.

joule   The unit of energy or work done: 1 joule of work done is when a force of 1 newton moves an object a distance of 1 metre.

kinetic energy   The energy that a body possesses because of its motion.

Lami's theorem   If three forces A, B and C act on a particle that is in equilibrium and the angles between these forces are a, b and c, then $\dfrac{a}{\sin A} = \dfrac{b}{\sin B} = \dfrac{c}{\sin C}$.

light inextensible string   A string of negligible mass whose length remains the same when a force is applied to it, whether motion is taking place or not.

light rigid tow-bar   A connecting rod of negligible mass, which does not change shape when a force is applied to it.

limiting equilibrium   When the frictional force is a maximum and equal to the pushing force; when an object is about to slip.

momentum   The quantity of motion that an object has, equal to its mass multiplied by its velocity.

newton   The unit of force: a force of 1 newton gives a mass of 1 kg an acceleration of $1\,\mathrm{m\,s^{-1}}$

Newton's first law   Every body remains in a state of rest or of uniform motion in a straight line unless an external force acts on it.

Newton's second law   The resultant of the forces acting on a body is equal to the mass of the body multiplied by its acceleration in the direction of that force.

Newton's third law   To every action there is an equal and opposite reaction.

non-conservative system   If work is done by an external force so that the total of the potential energy and kinetic energy of the system is not constant.

normal reaction   The component of the contact force exerted by a surface on an object that is perpendicular to the surface.

parallelogram rule   The sum of two vectors is geometrically represented by the diagonal of a parallelogram whose sides represent the two vectors being added.

particle   An object whose mass can be modelled as being concentrated at a point.

perfectly smooth   When there is no friction between two surfaces; the coefficient of friction is zero.

power   The rate at which work is done.

principle of conservation of energy   The total energy of a system remains constant provided no external work is done.

principle of conservation of linear momentum   For two (or more) interacting objects, not acted upon by external forces, the total momentum is constant.

pulley   A wheel over which a string passes.

resolve   Break up a force into its components in two perpendicular directions.

resultant   The single equivalent force when two or more forces act on a body.

scalar   A quantity that has magnitude (size) only.

sine rule   In a triangle ABC with sides of length a, b and c: $\dfrac{a}{\sin A} = \dfrac{b}{\sin B} = \dfrac{c}{\sin C}$.

smooth   When it can be assumed there is no friction between two surfaces.

smooth pulley   A pulley for which friction in the bearings can be ignored.

triangle rule   The sum of two vectors is geometrically represented by the third side of a triangle formed by placing the starting point of the second vector on the finishing point of the first.

vector   A quantity that has magnitude (size) and direction.

velocity   A vector quantity that tells us how fast a body is moving and in what direction.

velocity–time graph   A graph showing the motion of a particle in one dimension with velocity on the vertical axis and time on the horizontal axis.

watt   The unit of power: 1 joule per second.

weight   The force exerted on a body by gravity.

work done   The product of force and the distance moved by a body in the direction of the force.

work–energy principle   The total work done on a system is equal to the total change in energy.

Index